ALTERNATE FLIGHT PLAN

8/23/18

For Cristie —
May all your
flights be
fanciful !

[signature]

ALTERNATE FLIGHT PLAN

The Lost Diary of Amelia Earhart

As Shared by

LOIS P. FRANKEL, PH.D.

Copyright © 2018 Lois P. Frankel, Ph.D.
All rights reserved.
ISBN-13: 9780692992760
ISBN-10: 0692992766
Cover Design by Lisa Graves

Also by Lois P. Frankel, Ph.D.

Women, Anger & Depression

Kindling the Spirit

Overcoming Your Strengths

Nice Girls Don't Get the Corner Office

Nice Girls Don't Get Rich

Stop Sabotaging Your Career

Nice Girls Just Don't Get It (with Carol Frohlinger)

Ageless Women, Timeless Wisdom

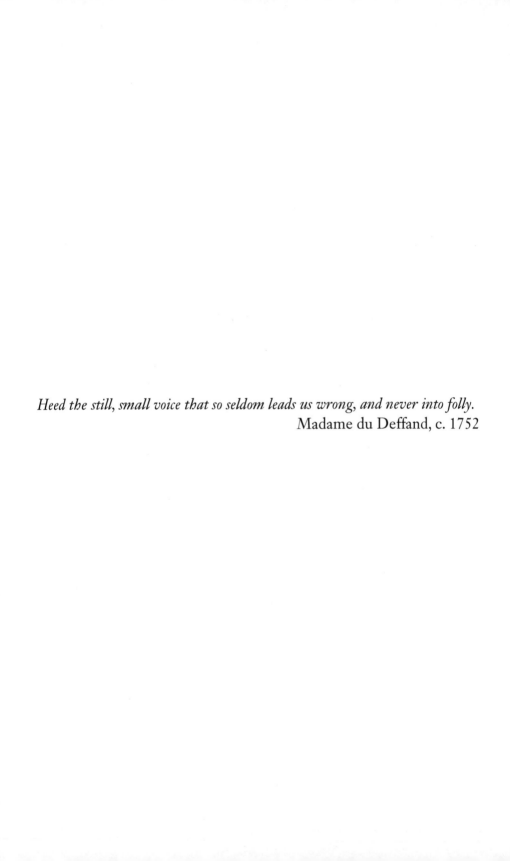

Heed the still, small voice that so seldom leads us wrong, and never into folly.
Madame du Deffand, c. 1752

INTRODUCTION

We never know the moment when our lives will profoundly change, never to return to the same shape or size in the same colors and hues with which they were previously painted. Sometimes it's a catastrophic event that transforms us. Other times it's witnessing great beauty or courage or kindness. What changed my life was a chance encounter with a woman I will never meet but who unknowingly sang my song. It began in August 2016, when I was handed a diary, yellowed with age and bound with twine.

"We will be landing in Jakarta in fifteen minutes where the local time is 10:25 a.m. Please turn off all electronic equipment and stow any items you may have taken out from the overhead bins. We realize you have a choice of airlines and thank you for choosing United," the weary flight attendant droned over the public address system. It was a long flight. I couldn't blame her for sounding less than enthusiastic. How many times had she uttered those exact words? How many times I had *heard* those exact words? How many more times would I hear them? The uneventful flight was what most travelers long for. For me, it provided a welcome respite from phone calls, e-mails, and texts and allowed me to reflect uninterrupted on my life. The past few years were a blur of flights, cities, clients, and an unfulfilling life at home. As much as I enjoyed meeting new faces and seeing new places it had come to the point they all ran together in my mind. If you asked me where I was last week, I would struggle to answer.

Yet I was living the life about which I had cautioned so many others. Like every other addiction, workaholics use their drug of choice (work) to avoid something unpleasant in their lives. Sometimes it's the loneliness of not having a relationship, sometimes it's the pain of being in an unsatisfying relationship. I really couldn't blame many of the workaholic men I knew who stayed long hours at the office because it was a socially acceptable way to delay going home to an unappreciative family. I also know it's a short-term solution to a long-term problem that eventually has to be confronted.

Friends have a romanticized view of my life. It seems exotic to people tethered to a desk from nine-to-five and who also bear the brunt of family responsibilities. And in many ways, it is a life quite out of the ordinary. One week I'm in Stockholm and the next in Hong Kong. Despite doing work I love, staying in five star hotels, and eating in the some of the finest restaurants in the world, I remain unfulfilled. I yearn for something I have no words to describe. Sometimes I wonder whether I would even know what I wanted if life delivered it to my doorstep. It's like the line from an old Barbra Streisand song, "I don't want much, I just want more."

Weary from twenty-four hours of traveling, I disembark from the plane to the familiar smells and sounds of Indonesia. Seeing the small, dark-skinned people brings a certain degree of familiar comfort. I have been going to Indonesia for nearly thirty years to conduct leadership training programs for oil company employees. The strong aroma of clove cigarettes fills the air. The smiles of the cordial Indonesian airline employees dressed in traditional batik garb who greet the arrival of the plane are always the same. I have the feeling that many of them don't feel like smiling, especially after all they've been through in the past years with political unrest, an economy spiraling downward, and natural disasters. But it is the Indonesian tradition to be gracious and welcoming. I appreciate their efforts.

Even in the climate-controlled environment of the airport, the air is thick with humidity. Condensation forms on the glass windows leading from the plane to the arrival area. From the jet way at Soeharto International Airport, I see the deep green foliage that grows to gigantic proportions from frequent rains. Just as a child grows before your eyes without your noticing the change, the thick vegetation surrounding the airport seems the same from year to year, but pictures that I took during my early trips here tell a different story. I pass the shops along the concourse filled with eye-catching jewelry, batiks, wood carvings, and souvenirs for last minute shoppers. I know the shops and their wares by heart. Mindlessly I make my way to passport control.

People unaccustomed to international travel often ask how I tolerate long flights halfway around the world. How can I possibly explain that they are often the only time I have to myself, free from the many people who tug at me with a constant barrage of questions and choices. The bigger ordeal is preparing to leave for a trip. Like so many other women, I am a wife, daughter, sister, friend, and professional woman. Add them up, and there are myriad responsibilities, none of which is too great but when combined can be overwhelming. I often find myself on automatic pilot, not living consciously, but rather surviving from moment to moment. A long plane ride is a gift of time.

Each time I board a flight I realize the relief of leaving it all behind. From the moment the car drops me off at Los Angeles International Airport I experience a sense of freedom – an unburdening of the weight that feels almost palpable on my shoulders. At times it precludes me from knowing what I would even *want* to be different. On the road I don't have to answer to anyone or meet the demands of being all things to all people. I only have to do my work, which at this stage of my career I do with the confidence that comes from repetition. Despite the oppressive heat and the smell of trash burning in nearby villages, walking through the concourse in Jakarta I can finally breathe.

Passing through immigration control, I make my way to the bank kiosk to change U.S. dollars into Indonesian rupiah. I notice the exchange rate is 12,000 rupiahs to the dollar. Fifteen years ago, it was 2,000 rupiahs to the dollar. I trade three hundred U.S. dollars for over three million rupiah. More than most people in this country will earn this year – or any year for that matter. As I count out the money given to me I hear my name being called.

"Lo-is!" Itje exclaims breathlessly running across the arrival area. "I am so sorry I was not here to greet you."

"But you are here," I laugh, encircling my arms around her small frame in a heartfelt bear hug. "Apa kabar, temen saya?" *How are you my friend?*

Itje takes my hand and we walk toward the luggage carousel and immediately begin chatting as if no time has passed since our last visit. Waiting for my luggage to appear she asks about my family, not in the least surprising in Indonesia – a country where family comes first. If you ask someone if they are married they will inevitably reply either yes or, "Not yet." Ask if they have children and you will get the same reply. In turn I ask Itje about her family, and she hands me her mobile phone with hundreds of pictures of her sons, grandchildren, and other friends and family members. I look at Itje and smile. She grins back at me. No words are necessary. We are both delighted to be in the presence of the other once more. Seeing each other only once a year makes each visit special and the depth of our connection does not require the kind of getting reacquainted that less intimate relationships necessitate. We have known each other almost have of our lives.

When we've retrieved my luggage from the carousel, Itje calls her driver and instructs him to pick us up at the curb. Inside the Kijang, she once again takes my hand and we ride a while in silence. The kind of silence reserved for old friends who feel no need to fill the space with idle chatter regardless of the time between visits. The drive through Jakarta has the familiarity of my own neighborhood. Having been here so many times, it's like coming home. I am no longer in awe of the machinations of this city rarely visited by Westerners except on business.

Racing past my periphery is laundry hanging on lines outside of shacks in the middle of swampland. On the road from the airport to downtown Jakarta, women squat to wash frayed clothing in the muddy water while children play in the squalor that is the norm for them. Tall office buildings and condos come into view in the distance. A juxtaposition of wealth and dearth. How odd that these sights and smells make me feel as though I am home and safe for at least some period of time. Friends and family in the United States warn me of the dangers of visiting this misunderstood country, but to me it is no different from going to another city in the U.S. – it just takes a little longer to get here.

"Itje, something is on your mind," I finally break the silence with a concerned observation. There is a long silence before she responds.

"I wanted to wait until you were rested after your long trip, but you know me too well," she starts. "I found something I think you should have," she starts. "It is about an American. An American who lived in Indonesia for many years."

The quizzical look on my face encouraged her to continue.

"You know that my mud-der was an herbal healer," she raised her eyebrows to confirm that I remembered this. When I nodded my head, she continued.

"When I was a very lit-tle girl she brought me to Subang to live with a woman who had taught her everything she knew about herbal medicine. The woman was a *bule*. We thought she was a missionary from the United States." Itje paused for a moment to be certain I was following her. She knew that I understand the word *bule* meant a foreigner. Again, I nodded listening carefully.

"The woman started a school and that is where I learned English. She was very kind, and my mud-der loved her very much," Itje paused once again.

"A very famous woman? Like how famous?" I asked.

"If I am correct, she is the woman thousands of people searched for after she disappeared in her plane in the Pacific Ocean," she said.

"You don't mean Amelia Earhart?" I said incredulously.

"You know of her then?" Itje asked.

"Sure," I replied as my mind quickly tried to access what I had learned about her from books and newspaper articles. "At least I know the basics of who she was."

"I believe it is her," Itje said.

"Why would you think the woman who taught your mother about herbal medicine was Amelia Earhart? That's a long-shot, Itje," I said doubtfully. "No one really knows what happened to her. There has only been speculation for decades."

"Because I met her. I talked to her," Itje said simply.

"You talked to Amelia Earhart?" My skepticism was tangible.

"Yes, I did," she said resolutely.

"How do you know it was her?" I asked.

"Because when I read what she left behind, I believed this was the woman I knew my whole life," Itje said with conviction.

"C'mon, Itje. You have got to be kidding me," I said.

"Yes, it's true," Itje began to explain. "Before she died she told my mud-der's friend, Tuti, where to find something very important to her. But Tuti could not read English and did not know what it was, so she just left it where it was for many years," Itje explained.

"So how did you find it, then?" I asked.

"As you already know, when I retired I was asked to take over the Amri School of English in Subang," she began. "One day I was cleaning out some file cabinets and came across a lot of papers tied up in a string. I started looking at them and realized they were written by the woman we all called Meely."

Meely, I thought. I seemed to remember reading somewhere that this is what Amelia Earhart's family called her.

"Go on," I said.

"In the papers Meely said her real name was Amelia Earhart. After I read them, I went to the Internet and looked for pictures of Amelia Earhart," she continued. "Although by the time I was born she looked very different, I could see a similarity. Then I asked everyone who was living with us in the 1970s if they knew anything about these papers.

Tuti told me she had seen Meely writing these papers and what Meely had asked of her. She was a lit-tle hesitant to tell me because she did not do what Meely told her to do. Still, I could not be sure. So I waited until I knew you would come here to ask you what I should do."

With this Itje pulled from a well-used colorful cotton batik tote bag a stack of yellowed papers tied in twine. Handing it to me she said, "Lihat itu." *Look at it.*

I laid the papers on my lap and gently untied the twine. It appeared to be a diary written long-hand in pencil on crude paper. There were no staples or binding. Just the twine held it together for all of these years. The brittle pages, already worn with time, had to be turned with the utmost care. The perfect penmanship and phrasing revealed the writer was likely someone educated in the United States in the early 1900s. It looked like something my grandmother could have written it, and she was born in 1901. Each page was marked in the lower left hand corner with the initials A. E.

And so began my incredible immersion into the life of Amelia Earhart. Each day after returning from the training center where I was working, I would set up shop in the Jakarta Hilton business center to meticulously research the dates, names, places, and stories contained inside this diary. Late into the night I would stay, cross-checking facts until the center staff had to ask me to leave so that they could close. Every so often I would pick up the phone to call Itje with a question about where a particular city was or if there was really a company with a specific name.

By the end of the fortnight that I spent in Jakarta, I could confirm certain facts. Sure enough, Amelia Earhart disappeared on July 2, 1937. Yes, her family name was Meely. Her father was indeed an alcoholic. She had worked at Spadina Hospital in Canada. She had taken Eleanor Roosevelt on an airplane ride. Each fact checked out. There was no way the person who wrote this could know all of these personal details of the life of Amelia when there was no Internet to conduct research and few (if any) books in Indonesia written about her life. Fact after fact checked out. There could be no doubt. Unless this was some very elaborate hoax, I was in possession of the diary of Amelia Earhart.

Before returning to the United States, I asked Itje what she would like to do with the diary. Entrusting me with the papers now rewrapped in the same twine as they were originally when handed to me, she asked that I take them to the U.S. and use my contacts in publishing to let the world know what really happened to Amelia Earhart. This was clearly what Amelia wanted – to put the myths to rest once and for all. And, although it could be my own filter coming through, I also believe she wanted to share her story so that other woman could learn from it. Without preaching or proselytizing, her explanation of the life that she chose to live after the crash of the Electra provides today's women with inspiration for examining their own lives and making choices that will bring fulfillment and joy to them. After reading, it I hope it makes a difference in your life and that you will agree Amelia always was ahead of her time.

THE FINAL FLIGHT

After so many years of hearing and reading stories speculating about my disappearance, I feel I must finally come forward before the facts are lost. It occurred to me many times before to recount my story, but, at first, paper and writing instruments were not available. What I took for granted living in the United States are luxuries for those living with less privilege. Much later, when the tools needed to capture my thoughts did become available, it seemed like sharing my story would only bring up painful memories and intrude on the new life I had created. Not only for me, but also for the people I know considered to be my family. I resisted writing about the past – the life I consciously chose to leave behind. In my folly it seemed that if I did not write about it, it did not exist. The thirty-nine years I lived before July 2, 1937, wasn't a bad life. Given the time for quiet contemplation I realized it simply was not the life I wanted.

Today I am an old woman in declining health. My doctors tell me that the cancer that started in my lungs has moved to other parts of my body. Given the choice of surgery that may or may not help, or living my life as independently as possible until my final incapacitation, I choose the latter. I've lived a full life. I am not sorry for my choices, and I am not afraid to die. Yet one of the few regrets that I do have is that I put so many people to such great inconvenience and caused my family such pain. Although one might believe that it brought me satisfaction in a perverse sort of way, it is in fact the last thing I would ever wish to do. Now, with the realization I have little time left, I wish to illuminate why I made the decision to live my life in obscurity rather than in the public eye.

I have neither the time nor the patience to write a detailed summation of my life. I prefer to share the touch points that define who I am today rather than focus on the person the public thinks of as Amelia Earhart. There seems to be no shortage of books available about my early life. I've read a few that I found in second-hand book shops. Some of them are even factually accurate. Then there are the books and articles that speculate about my disappearance. From theories about espionage to being stranded on a deserted island, people have certainly tried to get to the bottom of it all, and in the most creative ways. No, I have no need to dredge up the past. I simply want to set the story straight before it is too late.

I would be less than honest if I didn't say the thought of "disappearing" had not occurred to me before Noonan and I landed the Electra in the Pacific on July 2, 1937. The irony is not lost on me that two days before U.S. Independence Day I became independent for the first time in my life. Although the public saw the smiling, heroic Amelia, inside I felt continually besieged by responsibilities that were not of my making but nonetheless required my attention. Perhaps this too explains my love of flying, for in the sky the burdens of expectation were far away, and I felt the most marvelous sense of freedom as I soared like a bird without a care. After each flight, upon landing, I was once again faced with having to be that person others wanted me to be without truly seeing or caring about what was really important to me.

Even though I had thought about what life might be like out of the limelight, I did not at first think I had the strength and courage required to leave everything known and familiar to me behind. It took time to make the decision to live my life in obscurity. The fact of the matter is that I did not have much choice initially. When I was rescued and brought to a tiny remote village, I had neither the strength nor the means to let anyone know where I was. Over time I realized that despite the primitive living arrangements and the absence of close friends and loved ones, I was actually happy. Happier than I could recall being since the carefree days of childhood.

It may seem like an extreme measure, but I felt that I had finally found the means by which I could live my life the way I wanted, not the way others wanted me to live. It is never one big thing that causes us to make momentous decisions in our lives. It is more often the accumulation of hundreds of little things. It was also not without great consideration for loved ones, colleagues, and even strangers who expressed concern for my disappearance that I made my decision. The decision was not made capriciously or simply to capitalize on the opportunity of the moment.

I did not ask for attention to be paid to me as a woman aviator. As my reputation grew, I became increasingly uncomfortable. As flash bulbs popped and shutters clicked for photographs taken before my final flight, my discomfort was obvious, and I was impatient to begin my voyage. My husband George Putnam, or G.P. as he was known, insisted that I must be kept in the public eye to pay for what he referred to as my "flying folly." From luggage to lounging pajamas, G.P. lent my name and image to anything he thought would sell well. At one point he even signed a contract for me to appear in advertisements for modern kitchens! Why I never even learned to cook. I finally put my foot down one day and told him I simply would not honor a business deal he had made to put my name on ribbons attached to children's hats. That went one step too far for me.

Nor did I ever want to be a flag-bearer for women's rights. That was an honor – or imposition depending on how you view it – bestowed on me by others. It never occurred to me that I couldn't or shouldn't fly because I was a woman. And it never occurred to me that others couldn't do what they wanted simply because they were women. So when the headlines began to tout me as the first female doing this or that, I couldn't understand what all of the hullabaloo was about.

From the time I was in my late teens I wanted only two things. The first was to fly, and the second was to make a difference in the lives of others. Whenever possible I participated in projects that allowed me to do both of those (and preferably at the same time). I particularly enjoyed speaking on college campuses where I encouraged impressionable young women to pursue their dreams regardless of the pressure they received from a society determined to keep them engaged in activities deemed best suited for ladies. Shortly before my final flight, perhaps it was 1935 or 1936, I surveyed the women students at Purdue University where I was serving as visiting professor to find out what they planned to do after graduation. Although the findings did not surprise me personally given my own ambitions, it did raise eyebrows when others learned that over 90 percent of them wanted to earn their own livings. I delighted in encouraging them to take risks, pursue nontraditional fields, and find fun in whatever work they ultimately chose.

Over the years I have seen some of the pieces that writers, journalists, and others have concocted in an effort to put closure to a story that seemed to beg for a period, a last chapter, an ending – whether happy or not and whether accurate or not. I have also read biographies about me, which are oddly entertaining as they are written of one who has passed away, yet here I am, thousands of miles away from the writers, very much alive. Everyone had their own interpretation of my life, and I do not wish to dispute any view. Each writer put the pieces of the puzzle of my life together in the way he or she saw fit. In some ways, I think several of these authors understood me better than I understood myself. For the most part, what has been written about my life before my final flight is accurate and I have no interest in a detailed recitation of facts about my childhood or my family. That has already been well-documented.

I am a simple woman. I had a simple goal, and that was to fly. As I reflect back on my life over the past three decades, I recognize that in many ways it was unremarkable, yet I believe in this simplicity lies a message to other women who find themselves at a crossroads. How often do we have everything we could ever need but little of what we really want? Giving up those things that others assumed were important to me enabled me to find my true destiny.

This is not to say that giving up what is familiar and known to us is easy. There were days that I so longed to sit down and have a chat with my sister. Or to be in the sky once again. At other times, I would have paid a king's ransom for a good hot bath. Often, I questioned the sanity of my decision. But as the days, weeks, and years passed, I realized the very things that I missed were the same things that precluded my journey of self-discovery. There really was no other way. The more I gave away of my past, the more I was able to embrace and welcome both my present and my future.

THE CRASH

I find it difficult to write about the actual plane crash that changed my life. The event is fraught with memories that are painful to resurrect, yet I know it is a piece of my story that must be told. The date July 2, 1937 is indelibly etched into my memory. It was just three weeks before my fortieth birthday. Now it has been over thirty years since I was found floating at sea, dehydrated and near death. The combination of delirium and intervening years has caused me to forget many of the details of what truly happened during that period. The last thing I recall is flying with my navigator, Fred Noonan, toward Howland Island. We were already low on fuel when an unexpected storm whipped around our airplane. We tried desperately to contact anyone who might hear our distress signal. We could hear others, but they could not hear us. "Mayday! Mayday!" Noonan shouted into the radio. "Mayday! May Day!" I can hear the panic in his voice at this very moment just as if he were here next to me now saying it aloud.

As Fred tried to alert our ground staff about the location of our plane and get help with directions to our next stop, I tried to control the plane as it lurched through the wind and rain. We knew we were close to our destination but could not locate it. We flew in the thick pea soup and watched for the choppy waters below when it appeared momentarily through the clouds. What must have been hours seemed like minutes as we desperately sought either assistance or Howland Island – both of which were essential to our survival.

Neither of us wanted to be the first one to say so, but it was apparent we had no hope of finding land before our fuel supply was exhausted. With six fuel tanks carrying over 1,000 gallons of gas, we should have been able to fly for twenty hours under normal cruising conditions. These conditions were far from normal, and we had now flown for nearly eighteen hours since last refueling. The weather conditions and extended time in the air were quickly devouring our fuel. When the plane's engine began to sputter, Noonan and I agreed we had no choice but to land our plane in the ocean.

It was nearly dark when the Lockheed Electra made contact with the surface of the North Pacific Ocean. Halfway between Hawaii and Australia, our plane broke into pieces upon impact. We braced ourselves as the 6,000-pound plane slammed into the water at one hundred twenty-five miles per hour. By the grace of God, we did not lose consciousness. Although we were badly bruised with cuts and scrapes, and Noonan's left shoulder appeared to be dislocated, we were able to find a buoyant piece of fuselage on which to float. We intuitively knew to each cling to opposite ends in an effort to keep it balanced. My ears were ringing from the noise the plane made when it hit the water. Over the noise from the storm and the ringing, I could barely make out Noonan's voice two yards away from me. He was asking if I was all right. So like him to put his personal needs and his own pain in abeyance and to look out for me.

We drifted in silence. I was thinking about the ill-conceived decisions I had made earlier in our trip. To make the Electra lighter and, therefore able to fly further between refueling, I had insisted that we abandon the life vests. In retrospect, neither should I have removed the Morse code equipment and flares during our stop in New Guinea, the last place we refueled. But we had come 22,000 miles and had only 7,000 to go. Were we not just about home free? In retrospect, it's clear that these and other abandoned items could have helped us to find Howland Island or to have rescuers find us.

One always has a seemingly logical reason for making decisions in the moment, and second-guessing those decisions after the fact does no good. I do have deep regrets, however, that Noonan perished as a result of the decisions for which I must assume complete and total responsibility. He was a wonderful traveling companion and crackerjack navigator, despite what others have implied.

Both before and after our trip, I read commentaries that suggested Noonan was not the best choice as navigator for the journey. Some even went so far as to blame him for our disappearance. Nothing could be further from the truth. Every inch of the six-foot Noonan rose to the occasion, and he did everything possible to ensure our survival. He could be quite a scoundrel at times, much like the boy next door who would tease you mercilessly one moment only to help you fix your bicycle the next. But Noonan was a good man with a significant amount of flying experience, and if not for my pig-headedness he might be writing this story today rather than I.

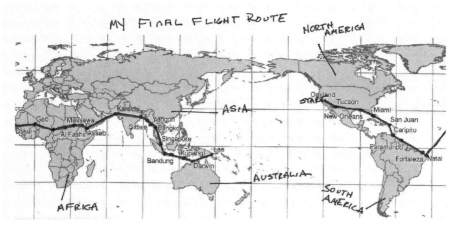

My Final Route

As strange as this may sound, that first night adrift at sea was actually quite peaceful. The storm had passed, and once the smoke from the crash cleared out we could see a bright half-moon that illuminated the ocean as far as the eye could see. The light dancing across the rhythmic waves belied the dire nature of our circumstances. The silence was in stark contrast to the constant humming and vibration of the plane's engine. We took turns sleeping and when awake expressed optimism that it would not be long before we were found. We foolishly underestimated the vastness of the ocean.

Dawn broke clear and warm. The storm that caused us to abandon the Electra had silently snuck away. Despite the pain he was in, Noonan's penetrating blue eyes twinkled as we spent the first two days exchanging stories about the first thing we would eat when rescued, what we would do upon return to the United States, and events from our childhoods that led us to this moment. Why had I never taken the time before to know Noonan the man and not simply Noonan the navigator? During periods of silence between us, I wondered about the number of other people I may have failed to see on a deep human level because I was so caught up in my own thoughts, my own project, and my own worries. Although I had been a nurse caring for the war wounded, and I had cared for my own family and friends in their times of need, this was not the same as seeing them. The former is doing and the latter is being. I knew all too well how to *do*, but I had failed miserably at *being*.

On the third day, Noonan exhibited symptoms of delirium, no doubt from being dehydrated and not having eaten for so long. I tried to keep him awake and alert by shouting his name and slapping his face with what little energy I had left. I sang to him and pulled his hand toward mine so that I could keep him aloft. The warmth of the sun and the gentle rocking from the waves must have caused me to drift off to sleep because when I awoke Noonan was gone. I looked around, hoping it had been only seconds and surely I would spot him nearby. I called his name, hoping for a return cry. But he was nowhere to be seen or heard. Darkness crossed my soul. A voice that sounded as if it came from me but over which I had no control yelled, "Nooooooooooooo!" I hung my head and cried. The burden of responsibility for Noonan's demise weighed heavy on my heart. It felt as though my heart sank into my stomach. A part of me left with him. A part that I would never regain. I truly believed I would soon be joining him. Crawling to the center of the fuselage to maintain balance I drifted in and out of consciousness.

As I sit here today recounting the experience that changed my life forever and took Noonan's, I know I am responsible for our fate. Noonan was a good friend and flying partner until the very end. I miss him to this day and wish he and I could have had one more successful flight together. Truth be told, I was never one to pay close attention to details and took too many risks in the sky. I had no patience with learning the complex intricacies of flying. It is not out of humility that I say I never considered myself a true aviator. I was a flyer. I understand my temperament. Like many things in my life, I focused on what was of most interest to me and ignored the rest.

This bad habit was first recognized by Mrs. Walton, my fifth grade teacher at the private school where Grandpa Otis enrolled my sister Muriel and me. I loved to learn, but Grandpa was not happy with the return on his investment in my education when Mrs. Walton sent home a note saying, "Amelia's mind is brilliant, but she refuses to do the plodding necessary to win honors prizes." Grandpa asked me why, if I could come up with the right answers, I couldn't explain how I arrived at them. I told him winning prizes wasn't important to me.

So many times over the years I would think, "If only I had…" – done this or not done that. But life doesn't always give us second chances. Although we know only in retrospect whether a decision is good or bad, we are always responsible for their ramifications. We cannot change them, but we can learn from them. We cannot fill the hole that is left when a decision results in loss, but we can forgive ourselves enough to continue to make a difference in the world. Changing the past is impossible, and creating the future is imperative.

On this cool, balmy evening in the mountains of Subang I am confronted with the reasons why I have not before told my story. It's painful to recall the events of so long ago. I pray that I have the inner strength to continue.

Rescue at Sea

N oonan and I were confident that we would be rescued. We were half right. Only one of us was to survive. The next thing that I recall after Noonan's death was awakening on a fishing boat with my scarf and leather coat torn, but still intact. As if it were yesterday, I remember the day I bought that coat and scarf. Wanting desperately to look the part of an aviator, I wore the coat to bed every night for a month to give it the appearance of being seasoned – even though I certainly was not. Ah, such are the foolish fancies of a young girl.

Despite the warmth of the day when I regained consciousness, I was chilled to the bone and glad for the outer layers of clothing. A lilting motion let me know that I was on a boat. At first I wondered if it was delirium, but the smell of fish and clove cigarettes was so real that I knew this could not be the case. My mind wandered back to the first time I had smelled clove cigarettes. It was when we stopped for repairs in Bandung, Indonesia. Back then it was simply called Java. I tried to lift myself from the makeshift bed only to fall backward with no energy to support my now frail body. There was no one around but I could hear the muffled sound of strange voices above deck. And seagulls. I could hear their cries and the flapping of what sounded like hundreds of pairs of wings. I did not know where I was or with whom. I tried to call out but fatigue allowed no sound to emerge. The wooden boat creaked with each gentle wave. It soon lulled me back to sleep.

When I awoke the second time, two small brown men with brown eyes and brown hair were standing over me. Each had smooth-looking skin devoid of facial hair except for a few wisps of hair extending from each man's chin. They spoke a language that sounded vaguely familiar but that I could not place. One of the men leaned down to give me a bit of water – slowly, in much the same way as one might feed a baby bird. They looked at me with curiosity but were at the same time gentle and kind. I was not afraid – only grateful. I managed to ask them who they were, but there was no reply. My voice sounded weak and raspy. I asked them where I was, but clearly they could not understand me. My eyes slowly began to close, and soon I was once again fast asleep.

I do not know how long I was on the boat before I regained full consciousness, but I counted twenty-two sunrises at sea before arriving on land. Combined with the time I had spent floating after the crash, I imagined it to be sometime in August.

I had been rescued by a fishing boat. The seagulls I had heard earlier were frantically circling above the boat, waiting for fish to escape the bulging nets that were being hauled onto the deck. About a dozen young men worked the nets, a middle-aged man navigated the boat, and an old man with no teeth cooked and cleaned up the boat. The cook stacked wooden crates to create a small private space for me below deck. Using rags and a tarp, the men fashioned a crude bed and pillow for me. Every so often, perhaps once every few hours, one of the men would come and check on me. In the morning, just before sunrise, and again when the sun was high in the sky they would bring me water and rice. When it became dark, they cooked some of the freshly caught fish over an open fire. They mixed the fish with rice and ate it with their bare fingers. The cook always made sure I received a small but quite sufficient share of the day's catch.

At first I was too weak to leave my little cubbyhole. I awoke for short periods only to fall back to sleep for even longer ones. After about two weeks, I regained enough strength to venture onto the deck. Initially, I would stay for only minutes then for increasingly longer periods, always careful to remain out of the way of the busy fishermen. The intense aroma of their clove cigarettes remains with me to this day. I can close my eyes and smell it wafting about.

Although the men spoke a language I could not understand, I did comprehend and appreciate the universal language of kindness. I tried to remember whether I was ever in a situation where I had exhibited this kind of uncommon generosity of spirit to a stranger. I could not recall one, but hoped if I were to find myself in such a position in the future that I would find it in my heart to do so.

On the day of the nineteenth sunrise, it seemed that the fishing expedition was complete and the men appeared to be preparing to sail for home. They packed up their gear and spent the days cleaning and drying their catch. They laughed and sang songs to pass the time. The atmosphere on the boat was lighter and more joyful than when they were hauling in the nets. Their work was done and now it was time to play. They even tried to teach me the words to a few songs, singing very slowly and enunciating the words carefully so that I might catch on. But this was a language I had never heard before. I could make out no familiar words nor could I imagine what they might mean. Even when I worked and studied in Canada for a short period of time I was able to learn French phrases. With no words to communicate, I spent hours alone with my thoughts for the first time in a very long while. I did not feel isolated. I felt fortunate to have this time all to myself with no responsibilities for anyone else, no projects to attend to, and no one trying to point me in a direction toward which I did not want to turn.

As the boat approached land I could see a small village with thatched huts surrounded by enormous trees. It looked like a dense jungle with an area carved out for a village. As we got closer to the shore, I recognized the foliage as being similar to what we had in California, but the leaves on the trees and bushes were ten times the size. The bamboo, unlike the skinny stalks surrounding my home in Los Angeles, was no less than a yard in circumference. The pothos leaves were the size of two breadboxes. Hundreds of palm trees laden with coconuts encircled the village. And trees with fruits that I had never before seen dotted the landscape throughout the village. It was a veritable Eden.

The boat was met by naked children swimming out to climb on board. They searched for and found their fathers and clung to them in a joyful reunion as if to let go would mean their loved ones would once again disappear for weeks. Women with well-worn, but colorful and clean saris hanging from their hips waited on the shore. Some held babies; others stood watching totally forgetting about the baskets on their heads filled with fruit. The women's huge breasts were unencumbered by clothing. Like the men, they were small and dark skinned. At the time I wondered if it was too hot for them to wear more clothing or simply not part of their culture. Now I know both to be true.

As several of the men helped me off the boat and I waded through the shallow water toward the shore, the women and children stared in awe. In retrospect I realized they had never seen a white woman before. And for how I looked, I must have appeared quite frightening to them. At five-feet eight-inches tall, I stood a full head or more above both the men and the women. My skin was still red and somewhat blistered from prolonged exposure to the sun. My hair had grown to below my ears, and although I could not see it, I could feel it was matted with particles of debris embedded in knots. With no need for my leather coat, I wore the pants and blouse, filthy and tattered--like something out of Robinson Crusoe--that I had been wearing at the time of the crash. The man who was navigating the boat said something to one of the older women and nodded toward me. Immediately she came over, took me by the hand and led me to one of the huts.

Obediently I followed to a one-room hut with a dirt floor, lit only by the sun's rays filtering in through the straw walls and roof. The shelter provided little relief from the burning sun and stifling humidity. The hut was built on stilts to preclude flooding during turbulent tides. Crudely made bamboo furniture hugged the walls. In the center was a large rough-hewn table surrounded by equally rough small wooden chairs, worn smooth in spots through years of use. The woman sat me down on one of the chairs and then left the hut. As I looked around, children peeked through the doorway with large brown eyes taking in the sight. I smiled and waved them in. With that, the older ones scattered, but several of the youngest ones who had not yet developed a fear of strangers were brave enough to venture in. Still weak, I picked up the smallest one and put her on my lap. She touched my blonde hair and stared into my blue eyes with wonder. After my long ordeal, it felt good to touch the warm skin of another human being and have my smile returned by this naked innocent. It made me think about my sister Muriel and how on cold nights we would huddle together in bed, the closeness of one body warming the other. There is something about skin touching skin that is soothing, especially when it is that of a young child in your arms.

When the woman returned, she had with her a wooden bowl filled with water and two pieces of cloth. She shooed the children away and silently used the smaller cloth to ever so gently wash those parts of my body not covered by clothing. Then, gesturing with her hands, she indicated I should remove my clothing. Unashamed, I disrobed, and she completed washing the remainder of my body. Picking up the larger flowered cloth she wrapped it around me, including my breasts, as a sari. With no words exchanged, because none were possible, the woman cared for me as she would one of her fellow villagers.

For the first time since I was a child, I was being taken care of, rather than being the one to take care of others. I willingly surrendered to the woman, and for the first time since I realized I had lost Noonan I cried. Leaning over me while I remained seated on the little chair, the woman held my head against her unclothed breasts as I was finally able to release weeks of unspoken fear, confusion, and exhaustion. It seemed the tears would never stop flowing. Perhaps the fact that I knew the woman would not understand anything I could have said in English allowed me to sob in silence. It was the most vulnerable that I ever recall being in my entire life. The feeling was alien to me. I was usually the one who was strong for others – so much so that I often could not access, let alone describe, my deepest emotions.

The woman's demonstration of selfless kindness is something that I will never forget. Even now, so many years later, the memory brings me comfort. I have since tried to be to others in need the kind of person this woman was to me in my moment of need. I don't know that I've succeeded, but I did learn that small acts make a big difference when the human heart is involved. Had I remained an airplane pilot, I'm not sure I would have learned the same lesson. For not only did flying bring me solace, it also separated me from people on the ground. It was a solitary activity, and in my selfish way I coveted my time alone in air. Being "grounded" suddenly had new meaning for me.

It was a long while before I collected myself enough to look the woman in the eyes with what I hoped she would know was gratitude. We sat together as the sun became low in the sky until finally she brought me to another hut. This one had apparently been abandoned by its previous dwellers, who I guessed had either left the village, died, or moved to a larger one to raise their family. It had a bed made of grass and straw covered with a worn cloth. A wooden bowl rested atop a table made from local trees. A hole in the floor served as a latrine. An iron cauldron was suspended with bamboo rods on a platform. . This was my new home. Over the years spent in the village, I was given the tables, chairs, and other household items those moving away could not take with them or no longer wanted. My small hut could not have been further removed from the luxurious home I shared with G.P. in Los Angeles, or even the one I grew up in in Atchison, Kansas, but it was mine. All mine. And it was a refuge. As small and sparse as it was, when I went to sleep at night I felt safe – safer than I had ever felt in my entire life.

Without creature comforts, or even what some might consider to be necessities such as running water and electricity, life was more vibrant than ever. For the first time since I was a little girl I could actually watch a sunset and be in awe of its beauty, I could taste the freshness of food shared with me by the villagers, and I could live my life unimpeded by the expectations of others, defined on my own terms.

The Village

The first few days in the village were awkward for both me and those around me. I tried to ease the discomfort by joining the women in their daily chores. I helped wash the clothes in water brought from the ocean in wooden tubs, assisted with the preparation of meals that consisted of fresh food cooked over outdoor fireplaces or boiled in cauldrons, feeding the chickens that wandered about the village, and tending to the babies. It took very little time to become entrenched in their routine. I felt an unusual sense of bliss in the simplicity of it all. Which is not to say my new life was easy. I missed my friends and family terribly. There were nights I would fall asleep, willing myself to keep a vivid picture of each of them in my mind's eye. As I grew older, their images never changed. Perhaps that is another one of the benefits of living in seclusion: one never sees family members age, become infirm, or die.

I never considered myself someone who needed a lot of people around me, yet, here, living in such close quarters among nearly two hundred men, women, and children, I was initially lonely. I suppose part of that was because I could not communicate with more than simple gestures, but another part was not having those I cared about within speaking distance. As much I used to complain that each time one of my family members would ring me it was to ask for something, we did share a special bond that I held close in my heart. I wondered whether I would ever see them again. I was torn. I thought I should try to find a way to let my presence be known to the world outside of the village.

Of course there was no obvious way to do that. There was no means of communicating with the rest of the world, no automobiles or even roads to take me from the village to – well, to where? Why, I didn't even know where on Earth this village was located!

Amelia Earhart, the woman so in charge of her life and her destiny was now at the mercy of others. I never could have imagined it would be so easy to relinquish control in such a strange environment. There were times I thought about leaving on foot, walking my way back to civilization, living on the abundant fruits and vegetables available in the jungle, but another part of me appreciated the new found freedom I was experiencing. In many ways, my new life was much more civilized than the old. How ironic that much of the world would describe my current existence as uncivilized when in fact it felt just the opposite. But for the comforts of the Western world to which I was accustomed, my new home suited me just fine.

The village was nestled into a dense grove of banyan, banana, coconut, papaya and belimbing (star fruit) trees. Huts were spread throughout the bush so as to give each family maximum privacy without sacrificing the safety of being close enough to keep an eye on one another. On one side of the village sat a rice paddy crudely irrigated with water from the sea. Except for the paddy area and the clearing along the beach from which the ships sailed, there were trees for as far as the eye could see. The lush green provided shelter from the burning rays of the sun and the thick, humid air. There were no roads, only paths created by foot traffic that led from one hut to the other and from the ocean to the village a short walk from the shoreline. And on the very edge of the village was a barn with a small wooden cart and a very old horse. Beyond that was a path just wide enough for the horse and cart to traverse.

The fishermen periodically departed from what I would later learn was called *kampung* (the village) on their sea journeys, and I remained behind with the women and children – the latter running around naked playing in the same muddy water used for bathing, washing clothes, and cooking. Most days were spent gathering fruit and harvesting the rice once it had turned a golden yellow color. In addition to learning the names of each of the one hundred villagers, I began to learn their language with simple words such as name (nama), thank you (teriman kasih), water (air), fish (ikan), rice (nasi) and children (anak). The rest of our communications were through simple gestures or drawing pictures in the dirt. I became proficient at reading body language. Smiles, tears, frowns, or a touch all comprise a universal language to which I became acutely attuned.

The villagers had a difficult time pronouncing my name so I reverted to the childhood name coined by my sister Muriel, <u>Meely</u>. I delighted each time a child would run into my hut shouting, "Meely, Meely melihat (look)!" as they showed me an unusual shell or seahorse found along the beach. Slowly I regained my strength and along with it the desire to be of more service to those who continued to treat me like an honored guest.

Of course there were no calendars, so I had no idea of the date I arrived, but based on my calculations of how long I could have survived at sea added to the time I spent on the fishing boat, I assumed I arrived sometime in August. I kept track of the days and months by the sunrises. Sometimes I wondered if anyone could possibly find me here, but I wasn't worried. There was no sense in worrying as there was nothing I could do about it. The more time that passed, I became even more certain that I never wanted to be found. With renewed energy I began to feel the same sense of freedom that I did as a child on my grandparent's compound in Kansas. The women showed me how to cook simple dishes over outdoor fires. One of the women made me a sarong that matched her own. She was very proud. I was very honored. Soon I began to make my own clothing with a great sense of satisfaction. It made me realize how much I took for granted as an American.

My parents were not wealthy, yet I grew up wanting for little. Grandpa Otis was rich by standards of the day and always seemed to provide us with the extras that Papa, the proverbial ne'er-do-well, could not afford. Both he and Mother would rather that Muriel and I had joyful and interesting experiences than have money in the bank. In contrast, the stark existence I now experienced would be described by some as primitive, but to me it opened new doors and ways of thinking. I did not feel sorry for myself. I considered myself one of the luckiest women in the world. I was alive, surrounded by kind and loving people, and did not feel the layers of responsibility that weigh down so many others.

COURAGE AND PEACE

Today marks thirty-four years since my final flight. In a few weeks, I will be 74 years old. In the university psychology courses I took, I remember it being said that approaching anniversary dates brings a flood of emotions and thoughts. I'm sure this also plays a role in my desire to capture my story now. It is not with nostalgia that I write about the second half of my life, but rather with a sense of awe over the marvelous journey that I have taken. What others may consider harrowing, I consider an adventure. Is there any other way to look at life than just that – an adventure? We never know from day-to-day, indeed from moment-to-moment, what course our lives will take, what obstacles will be thrown into our paths. The adventurer makes the most of each and courageously steps into tomorrow.

It was always a curiosity to me that I became the representative of women in the sky. It was not a distinction I sought, nor one that I welcomed. I am not too proud to admit that I was never a student of aeronautics. I was simply enamored with the freedom it provided to me. Perhaps if I was more of a student of the sky I would have learned those things necessary to prevent the crash of my Electra. But to what end? Many times while living in Los Angeles I felt as if I was merely surviving – certainly not thriving. And living here in my adopted country I finally felt that I was thriving, despite the fact that I have had none of the accoutrements typically associated with a rich life.

What does it mean to thrive? For me, it means being able to live my life true to my values. Before I became Amelia Earhart, "darling of the skies," I was just plain Amelia, social worker. I often think back to the two years I spent in Boston living and working at Denison House as a teacher and home visitor to poor immigrants. I was in charge of the girls under fourteen. They were two of the happiest years of my life. I was making a difference. I even combined my love of work with my love for the sky by flying over the neighborhood and dropping leaflets to inform residents of the services provided by the social services community.

Denison House provided me with the stability I needed to explore the limits of my interests and proclivities. Much of my paycheck went to flying lessons and my spare time was spent writing. How odd that I cannot recall where I went last week, but can recite every word of a poem I wrote while at DH:

Courage is the price that life exacts for granting peace,
The soul that knows it not, knows no release
From little things:
Knows not the livid loneliness of fear,
Nor mountain heights where bitter joy can hear
The sound of wings.
How can life grant us boon of living, compensate
For dull gray ugliness and pregnant hate
Unless we dare
The soul's dominion? Each time we make a choice, we pay
With courage to behold restless day,
And count it fair.

It's not easy for a woman who is different. One who longs for more than social upbringing allows, yet wants to make her mark on the world. Even today, we are limited by social rules, family expectations, and personal conflict. Although I am sequestered from the modern world, I still make an effort to understand what is happening outside my limited sphere of existence. People write that I was ahead of my time. I don't know that this true. How could I be ahead of my own reality? Instead, I believe that women must listen to their internal voices and make choices that serve them well. We must learn to live in gratitude, not servitude.

In my case, that choice was to live a life of anonymity while still making a difference in the lives of others. Could I have better served the world with more notoriety? Perhaps, yes. But we must make choices that best suit our unique personalities and needs. As Robert Frost wrote not long before my disappearance, "Two roads diverged in a wood and I – I took the road less traveled by and that has made all the difference."

Dengue Fever

The years I spent living in the tiny fishing village, which I came to learn was called Buyat Bay, passed quickly. Despite the fact that Noonan and I had stopped for refueling in Bandung just weeks before, it wasn't until much later that I realized I was in the country of Indonesia. The native people looked familiar, but my Western eye was not able to distinguish between Indonesians, Philippinos, Thais, or Malans. The clue to me should have been the clove cigarettes! How the Indonesian men loved to smoke those cigarettes.

I kept track of the days that passed by scratching out sunrises on the trunk of a banyan tree just outside my hut. I later learned the banyan tree is part of the coat of arms of the Republic of Indonesia. One day melted into the next as I made myself useful attending to the children, teaching English to anyone who wanted to learn, and showing the women how to create more sanitary living conditions by boiling water and keeping eating utensils clean. For the first time in many years, I felt as if I was making a real difference to someone other than just myself.

Life in the village had a sense of order. Everyone had a role to play and everyone was important to the overall functioning of the community. Much the same as on a plane, there were tasks that needed to be performed and those who were most adept at the task did them. The strongest men built new huts and harvested trees; the elderly cared for the children and did chores that could be completed seated. And once a child was old enough, he or she collected eggs or picked the fruit for breakfast.

I was eager to contribute my skills along with the others. One of the things I most liked doing was singing the babies to sleep with lullabies I remembered from my childhood. Yet another lesson that there are universal languages that have nothing to do with the actual words. A melody hummed, a smile in passing, the touch on a shoulder – all communicate in ways that words sometimes cannot. And in these ways, and more, I had rich connections with my new friends.

What to some outsiders might look like a primitive, perhaps even barbaric, culture was actually a flourishing community built on mutual dependence, nurturing, and caring. Competition was unknown to these people. In its place, cooperation forged strong bonds in an atmosphere where what was good for one was good for all. This is not to say there weren't minor skirmishes. Jealousy, the most human of all emotions, would rear its head if a man thought his woman was spending a little too much time with another man. Or, if a woman thought she was working harder than the woman standing next to her, she would certainly say something. In most cases, just a look or a cold shoulder would remedy the situation. Living in close quarters with other human beings will do that. Your survival depends on others and vice versa in a way Westerners have never quite learned. It may not have been by choice, but my immersion into this society so foreign to me was an education I could not have otherwise received.

Approximately six months after my arrival, the village suffered from torrential rain storms, which dramatically increased the mosquito population in the village. Nearly half of the children and one quarter of the women of the village died from dengue fever. Mosquitos carrying the disease did not discriminate by age or sex. One bite from an infected mosquito could bring on a dangerously high fever along with an intense headache and an angry rash. The debilitating joint pain accompanying the disease caused the villagers to call it demam patah tulang (breakbone fever). My Red Cross training and work at Canada's Spadina Military Hospital during World War I was useful in limiting the number of casualties. Although there were no drugs to give these poor souls,

I knew enough to keep them hydrated and comfortable until they could heal – or die.

With many of the children left motherless, and the mothers who were left overburdened with the additional tasks that befell them, I helped build what might be called an orphanage. With assistance from the men when they returned from their fishing excursions, the necessary trees were cut down, and we fashioned a large structure with furniture brought in from huts emptied due to the destructive path of the disease. In the still of the night, the sound of whimpers of children crying out for their ibu (mothers) was heartbreaking. We would try to comfort them as best we could, knowing that we would never take the place of their loving parents.

Together with the women who remained, I helped to feed and educate the children, and most importantly make certain that none was without love. Before going on my final flight, G.P. and I talked about having children when I returned, but I never felt that I would make a particularly good mother. Nor did I think G.P. had strong paternal instincts. I considered myself too selfish and absorbed in my own endeavors to assume responsibility for nurturing anyone else. Perhaps I needed a crisis to recognize my maternal abilities and leanings. In a crisis, I always rose to the occasion. Mother, Papa, Muriel –and later G.P. – could always count on me to provide what they needed.

In the village decimated by disease, I quickly assumed the role of nurturing parent, even if I did not give birth to these children. I fed the ones too little to feed themselves, tended to the older ones when they got hurt, and tightly embraced the ones mourning the loss of a mother, father, sibling, or grandparent. In return, I received love that I did not know was possible. Sometimes I wondered who needed whom more or who gave more to whom. I learned the meaning of unconditional love. I only wish it did not take a plague to teach me the lesson. To this day, I feel that I received so much more than I ever gave during those difficult days.

Living so close to the equator, one cannot keep track of the months by the seasons. Each day eases into the next with little change in the hot, humid weather except for the arrival of the rainy season. Those who can speak English call the rainy season the "ber" months: September, October, November and December. After a while I stopped tracking the days on my banyan tree and instead kept track of the time based on the annual rains. I lost track of what month it might be and had no idea of what the day was. For someone who had lived her life so closely attached to a daybook, it was at first disorienting to be unable to identify the day of the week. But as the years passed, it was actually liberating. Why does one have to live her life tethered to a timepiece? We spend so much time worrying about if we are late to our next engagement that we fail to fully appreciate the moment in front of us. I believe this experience is magnified for women who are traditionally the ones to carry multiple responsibilities with little assistance from others.

This sense of liberation outweighed any feelings of isolation. I did think of my family and friends in the United States often. I wondered whether they had given up hope of finding me or continued the search knowing that if there was a way to survive I would. But as time passed and my bonds with the people in the village grew deeper, my longing to return home became fainter. It was not that I loved them any less, but that I loved my new life more. Surely there will be people reading this who cannot fathom the manner in which I made peace with my circumstances. And as they continue reading they will find even less understandable the direction I went once choices became available to me.

I was living in Buyat Bay for over three years when I saw the first people from outside of the village. I believe it was 1940 or 1941. After feeling safe and protected from the outside world for so long I suddenly felt fearful. Who were these people, and would they recognize Amelia Earhart? The first day I stayed in my hut, not wanting to risk being discovered. I knew I would stand out among the natives and did not want to risk the inevitable questions that would ensue. The villagers protected me, even the little ones by bringing me food and water.

Finally, I could not stand being cooped up any longer. I asked one of the women who these visitors were and learned that they were from a mining exploration company. I instructed the woman to tell them, if asked, that I was a missionary here to educate the children.

When I finally exited my hut on the fourth day after the visitor's arrival, I introduced myself to the men as simply Meely, a Christian missionary. By now my hair had grown long and I wore it tied up in a bun in the same style as that worn by the other women in the village. With brown skin, wearing a sarong and at least ten pounds heavier than I was at the time of my disappearance I prayed that I no longer resembled the Amelia who appeared in newspapers and magazines years ago. Although they looked at me with curiosity, they had no real interest in me or my work. They were after gold, and if I could not help them to find it or mine it I was of no use to them.

Listening to the men speaking English – with a British accent – did make me a bit nostalgic. It had been so long since I'd heard fluent English spoken by anyone other than myself. Teaching English to the children wasn't the same as hearing words confidently put together into sentences. Although it wasn't often that I thought about "home" it caused me to wonder what it would be like to go back to my old life. I recall an overwhelming feeling of sadness at the thought. It was as if hearing English transported me back to an existence now so foreign to me yet at the same time painfully familiar.

That night lying bed, I wondered whether it was time for me to return to America. The opportunity was here. Yet I knew that I would not, *could not*, return to my life as it was. As much as I loved Muriel, the children, and Mother, caring for them had become a constant worry and financial burden. When I paid off Papa's debts and house in California so that he could die in peace I thought that would be the end of it. But after his passing everyone looked to me to solve their problems, not the least of which was money. In marrying Albert, Muriel had found a man as irresponsible as Papa. He could barely provide for his wife and children let alone help to support Mother who could not possibly survive on her own. The three of them had come to count on my monthly checks for even their most basic needs. Although I did not resent sharing my good fortune with them, I did wonder what would happen to them if the well ran dry. Truth be told, I loved my life in Buyat Bay. What it lacked in glamour and luxury, it more than made up for in serenity and in endowing my life with meaning. Not only did the village need me, I needed the village.

AMRI

I loved all of the children in the village, but one in particular won my heart and forever changed my life. Amri was only five years old when his mother died; that same year his father failed to return from a fishing voyage. He was too young to understand what had happened, but it was clear that he suffered greatly from the loss. He no longer played with abandon in the muddy waters of the village. Instead, he stood by the edge of the shore watching the other children and looking out to the water as if waiting for his parents to return. At night he would leave his bed in the orphanage and crawl into bed with me. I would sing quietly to him until he fell back to sleep.

Soon Amri was living in my hut, a child eager to please and not wanting to let me out of his sight for fear that I too might abandon him. Little did he know that he was never far from my sight either. He would be by my side as I dried rice or cleaned fish, carefully watching as I went about my chores. Despite the fact that he was younger than the other children in my English class, he listened attentively until one night before falling asleep he looked up at me and said in perfect English, "Good night my Meely." Good night my Meely. My heart ached. I hadn't heard those words since Muriel murmured them so many decades past as she and I huddled together in our bed at Grandpa and Grandma Otis's house in Kansas.

Ever so gradually, Amri and I became a family. It was different from my family in the U.S. As much as I loved each one of them for who they were, we were brought together by serendipity. We were together because we were *supposed* to be. Amri and I were together because we *wanted* to be. We loved each other in a deep and special way I had never before experienced. I worried about him in a way I had never worried about another human being. I wasn't simply responsible for him, I was devoted to him. When I looked into his big brown eyes, seemingly too big for his tiny little face, I saw the potential that lives in every child. I wondered if I could give him a better life if I found a way to return to the United States.

The villagers seemed to not only accept this arrangement, they encouraged it. Looking back, I wonder whether they knew better than I did that I need someone of my own. When I was invited to a hut for dinner, Amri was invited too. When the older children went for long walks in the woods, they would ask my permission for Amri to join them. If I were to believe in reincarnation, I would say that Amri and I had lived another life together as mother and son. It was as though we knew one another on a deeper and more spiritual level than could be explained by our time together in the village.

Nearly a year after Amri came to live with me in my hut, he was stricken with a debilitating fever. But it was not accompanied by the other symptoms of dengue so I was puzzled as to what it might be. Keeping him inside the hut, hydrating him with water, and feeding him small bits of rice, I was thankful when he would eat just a few morsels. Despite my best efforts the fever persisted and he soon stopped eating. By now, the men developing the mines were ever-present, coming and going with regularity. Amri needed more help than I could provide to him. He needed real medical attention or surely he would waste away to nothing. I could not let him die. I could not love him any more if he had come from my own womb. He was my son.

When Amri's condition worsened, I went to one of the developers to ask for help. I explained that Amri was very ill and asked to be taken to the nearest town with a doctor. The man, having no interest in helping Amri or anyone else in the village unless it would benefit him, told me it would be several days before he would leave again. Several days!

Amri would be dead by then. I tried to persuade him to just come into the hut to look at the boy (hoping there would be some degree of compassion that might change his mind), but he would not be convinced. I frantically approached several other men only to be met with the same response. I must say that my opinion of the British was never the same after that. Unlike the warm reception I received from the British upon flying across the Atlantic for the first time, these men had no concern for the villagers or this sick little boy. They were only concerned with what they could get from their land.

With no choices left, I did what I had to do. Waiting until everyone was asleep to execute my plan, I bundled Amri into a crudely sewn thin cotton blanket and carried him to an open top, green Jeep with the keys left in the ignition. After placing him carefully in the back seat I climbed into the driver's seat and with courage unlike that needed for any of my flights, I turned the key and took off. Where I was going I did not know, but I had to get help for Amri. It was my first time in a motor vehicle in over three years but I had not forgotten how to operate the manual transmission. Thinking back, it was a foolish act performed out of desperation.

Knowing that the developers had gotten drunk on whiskey every night, I prayed that they were passed out, or at least disoriented enough to give me the head start I needed to find help. My prayers were answered. It was a dark, moonless night as I traveled along the one dirt road leading out of Buyat Bay and into the overgrown jungle. Despite my unfamiliarity with the road and the vehicle, I kept my eyes glued to the path I was on and followed the tracks left behind by vehicles that preceded me. With no mirrors in the vehicle, I kept looking over my shoulder to see if anyone was following. Every so often I would stop the Jeep to give Amri water. His labored breathing propelled me to climb back behind the wheel and drive even faster.

It was the most terror-filled night of my life. Even floating at sea after the crash did not compare to the horror of thinking Amri might die. I had no idea how close the nearest town might be or whether the

British men were in pursuit to their vehicle. None of that mattered. Amri's condition was worsening by the minute. Adrenaline fueled me to find help for my sick boy.

Marriage to G.P. Putnam

What a restless sleep it has been the past few nights. Writing this diary, conjuring up images and memories of so long ago, is even more painful than I would have imagined. I dreamt that G.P. had found me at Buyat Bay and took me back to Los Angeles against my will. The villagers were no match for his forceful insistence. In the dream I saw myself being driven away in a Jeep, looking back at my chosen family as they helplessly stood and watched. As I looked out the back of the vehicle at the group getting smaller and smaller with each meter we moved along the dirt path, I became more and more despondent. I sat silently beside G.P. with no words exchanged between us. When I was awakened by the mosque's morning call to prayer, I was relieved to find that it was only a dream.

Many people wondered why I married G.P. I knew why. He provided the answer to my financial worries. From the beginning, I knew that I had made a deal with the devil. Although he appeared to want to help me sate my ever-increasing obsession to be in the sky, he in fact wanted the reflected glory received from my accomplishments. G.P. was not a bad man, just a misguided one. Many people do not know that G.P., George Putnam, was from the famous Putnam publishing family. In retrospect, I realize how difficult it must have been to be the son of one so successful. In his efforts to prove himself a success in his own right, he constantly overcompensated, reaching for goals that were not personally important to him, but that would make him appear successful in the eyes of his family. Like so many of us, G.P. was not exempt from the demons from our past with which we must contend.

Yet even in marriage I wanted to keep my options open. I wrote a letter to G.P. the night before our wedding, February 7, 1931. I don't know how, but after my disappearance it surfaced and was published in a magazine in the 1950s.

                                                    Noank
                                                    Connecticut

                    The Square House
                    Church Street

Dear GPP

        There are some things which should be writ before
we are married -- things we have talked over before -- most of
them.

        You must know again my reluctance to marry, my
feeling that I shatter thereby chances in work which means most
to me. I feel the move just now as foolish as anything I
could do. I know there may be compensations but have no heart
to look ahead.

        On our life together I want you to understand I
shall not hold you to any midaevil code of faithfulness to me
nor shall I consider myself bound to you similarly. If we can
be honest I think the difficulties which arise may best be avoided
should you or I become interested deeply (or inpassing) in anyone
else.

        Please let us not interfere with the others' work or
play, nor let the world see our private joys or disagreements.
In this connection I may have to keep some place where I can go to
be myself, now and then, for I cannot guarantee to endure at all
times the confinement of even an attractive cage.

        I must exact a cruel promise and that is you will let
me go in a year if we find no happiness together.

        I will try to do my best in every way and give you that
part of me you know and seem to want.

                                        A.E.

36

Santi

Dawn was breaking when Amri and I finally reached the small town of Kamanta. By now the road had grown wider and the thicket of jungle had cleared. Horses and carts lined the sides of the road, smaller roads veered off in all directions. The sun was rising into a hazy sky. People were walking along the road. I could hear the morning call to prayer coming from a tiny mosque. I pulled to the side of the road toward a group of men with woven skull caps and long saris. They looked at me strangely. The sight of a white woman climbing out of a Jeep rendered them speechless.

As if it were yesterday, I recollect how I implored them for assistance, pointing to little Amri in the back seat. "Anak yang sakit," sick boy I cried. They carefully walked over and peered in, looking back at me. I told them the little boy needed a doctor. With this, all but one of the men in the group stepped back. The man who remained reached in and hovered over Amri. He was old with long white hair and some sparse chin hairs. With the back of his weathered hand he felt Amri's cheek. He put his head to Amri's chest and listened for a moment. Then silently the old man lifted him out and began carrying him down the road. The other men continued walking toward the mosque and I followed to a house on a nearby side street. There he laid Amri's limp body down on a musty smelling old couch and pulled a small worn suitcase from beneath a table. When he opened it I saw ointments and jars with handwritten labels containing what appeared to be herbs. I could not believe my good fortune! This man was a healer of some kind.

Carefully choosing jars labeled LEBAH SERBUK SARI (which I would later learn is bee pollen), BOSWELLIA (frankincense), and ECHINACEA the man measured an amount of each equal to about a tablespoon and mixed them into a small pot of water. Then he took the concoction and put it over a small wood burning stove stirring it slowly until it came to a boil. We stood awkwardly together looking down at Amri as we waited for the mixture to cool. Then he gently lifted Amri's head and helped him to drink it. When that task was completed he briefly left the room we were in and came back with another jar – this one filled with a paste that smelled like camphor – and began rubbing it onto Amri's chest.

Speaking to me in broken English the man said that he was going to prayer and would be back soon. He instructed me to keep feeding the tea to Amri, little sips at a time. I followed his instructions keeping a vigilant eye on my precious boy. It was then that I realized Amri was not just another little boy. Just as I was his Meely, he was my Amri. We were bound together, not out of blood but out of a deep love that would last a lifetime. Although I was never a religious woman, that morning I got down on my knees next to Amri, bowed my head and prayed that if there was a God he would spare the life of my child.

Returning from the mosque, the man continued speaking to me in broken English, but when I replied in Indonesian he shifted to his own language. While we kept watch over Amri, I learned that he was a medicine man who had learned his craft from a Chinese traveler who had once stayed in the town. His name was Santi, and he lived alone in this very modest house that to me, after years of living in a hut, seemed like a castle. His wife had died a number of years ago, and his children had moved away to study and work in Jakarta. I introduced myself as Meely, a Christian missionary. He asked few questions, for which I was grateful. He did not feel the need to fill the silence, nor did I. Together we sat on the floor at Amri's side waiting for his fever to break. Before leaving for midday prayer, Santi heated a fresh batch of the herb concoction and gently fed it to Amri. Then he stood and left the house once more.

Leaning against the little couch I closed my eyes just to rest them for a bit but soon I drifted into a deep asleep.

Just as the sun was beginning to set I was startled awake by the honking of horns. I had completely forgotten about the Jeep that I left abandoned by the side of the road. The British developers would certainly be angry and come searching for their vehicle. Santi could see the fear in my eyes as my head cocked listening to the voices getting louder as they approached his house. He walked outside while I peered carefully out the window covered only with a dirty piece of cloth. I could not see him as he moved slowly around the corner toward the sound of the men. Voices rose and fell as the men questioned the villagers trying to find out who had stolen their vehicle. Soon I heard engines starting and the humming of both vehicles gradually growing fainter. I heaved an audible sigh of relief. Back inside Santi explained that when he told the men that he did not know who had left the Jeep on the side of the road, the other villagers joined in professing their ignorance as well. Santi came and sat next to me, saying nothing. Once more, I was grateful and relieved to be rescued by the kindness of strangers.

A New Family

Santi invited me to stay with him as Amri slowly gained back his strength. People from the town sought Santi's help in healing ailments of various sorts. Each would stare at me in wonderment – the first time many had seen a booleh (white woman). I assisted Santi by fetching water, keeping the stove filled with wood, calming scared children, and comforting concerned parents. With each passing day Amri became increasingly animated. Within a few weeks he was tentatively venturing out of the house to play with the other children of Kamanta. The crisis had passed.

Santi made us feel welcome in his home. In the evenings once Amri fell asleep on the couch that had become his bed, Santi and I would talk. After living in remote Buyat Bay for so long I couldn't help but barrage him with questions – beginning with the details of our location and the areas that lay beyond Kamanta and Buyat Bay.. With the exception of the few who came to town to sell fish and fruit, most of the people of Buyat Bay had never strayed further than they could walk from the village.

From Santi I learned that I was on the island of Sulawesi. He pulled a frayed book from a shelf and pointed to a map of Indonesia, then to Sulawesi. I scoured the map looking for Buyat Bay but could not find it. He showed me a small bay at the south end of the Minahassa peninsula. Finally, he pointed to the town of Manado and indicated this was the largest town to where we now were. I finally had a mental image of where I was in relation to the rest of the world.

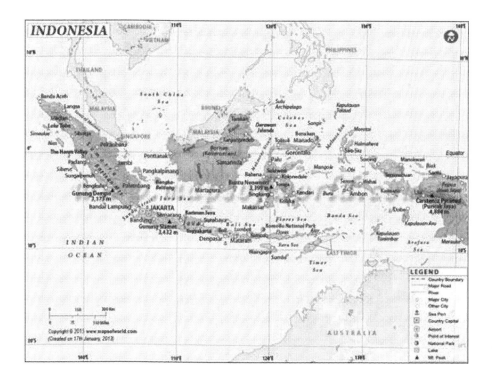

Another revelation was seeing myself in the mirror for the first time in many years. I had seen my reflection in the water of the village but not so clearly as now. My skin was lined in ways it had not been before. My hair was turning white. I no longer looked like the jaunty aviator in her overalls. I was a middle-aged woman who had spent years in elements to which she was unaccustomed. Unlike the dark-skinned natives, the sun took its toll on my fair skin. Fortunately, I was not vain.

Compared with the tiny fishing village where I had lived for the past years, Kamanta was a bustling town. The homes were a step above the huts in Buyat Bay. Still crudely made with dirt floors, they did have wooden walls, small rooms, and tin roofs. Of course there was no running water or indoor plumbing, but I experienced a new found sense of freedom in the spaciousness of the town. Once people became accustomed to seeing the booleh who lived with Santi, I could wander about without being disturbed.

I learned that it was February 1941. Santi kept a small self-made calendar and crossed off each day before he went to bed. Sometimes he would make a note on the calendar of something he wanted to remember to do or someone he wanted to check in on. I had been gone from the United States for three and a half years. And now I was worried about another home from which I had mysteriously vanished – Buyat Bay. I felt guilty about leaving so abruptly after all they had done for me. I wondered what they must think of me. If only I could let them know we were all right.

How curious that I felt I owed the villagers of Buyat Bay more than I owed my family and friends in the U.S. Perhaps it was because these people who had rescued me and nursed me back to health gave so much and expected nothing in return. They had become the family of my choosing, not the one into which I was born. It made me realize that the saying "blood is thicker than water" is not always true. Fate delivers us into our biological families, but we are free to create alternative families that nurture us in ways that are unimaginable--and at times, in ways we did not even realize we needed.

After six weeks living with Santi, feeling I could no longer impose on his generosity, I brought up the subject of returning to Buyat Bay. I did not know how I could get back to the village but felt it was time to leave, despite the fact that in a short period of time I had grown to enjoy my conversations with him and the exposure to a broader community of people. He listened as I explained the reasons why I thought it time to go and, after a moment of reflection, he presented an alternative.

Santi told me he was about to enter into his eighth decade, old by Indonesian standards of the time. He did not know how much longer he had to live and that he was worried about who would care for the people of Kamanta once he was gone. He said that watching me with the villagers who came to him for help made him realize that with a little training I could become a healer if I wanted to. The proposition was that I remain living with him and he would teach me herbal medicine. Santi said that he would pay me what he could and that he would arrange to get a message to the Buyat Bay villagers that Amri and I were fine.

As attractive as his offer was, I felt torn. What about the orphanage? The things I was teaching the children? What I owed to the people who had rescued me? I expressed these concerns to Santi, and he suggested that we look into getting another missionary to take my place. He did not know that I was not really a missionary or how the people of the village had saved my life. I struggled with whether I should tell him the truth, go back to the village, or remain in Kamanta.

That night I went to bed with a heavy heart. I did not consider myself a selfish person or one who did not live up to her obligations. Yet I had already selfishly abandoned one family. What would it say about me if I deserted yet another? I thought back to the conversations I used to have with Eleanor Roosevelt. We had so much in common – in her I felt I had found a kindred spirit. We would talk about our unusual childhoods without self-pity but pride for having overcome obstacles. The First Lady also shared my adventurous spirit coupled with a desire to help those less fortunate. I actually felt a bit sorry for her – burdened to a far greater degree than I with the imposition of having such a high-profile position. I wondered what Eleanor would do in the same situation. I had no doubt she would never have disappeared to begin with!

Eleanor had a strong sense of duty and loyalty. Why, she would not disobey the president's wishes even when she most wanted to! After she mentioned that she would love to have a flying lesson, I arranged one for her. It was something she was so looking forward to, but President Roosevelt squelched the idea by saying it was far too dangerous for him to permit. Instead, I took her on an evening flight over Washington, D.C. Although I know she enjoyed it, it was a far cry from flying on her own. Eleanor was one of the people I most missed in my new life. Had I returned, I believe we would have become the best of friends. When newspapers became available to me, I eagerly read about her many philanthropic endeavors. When I read of her passing in the 1960s, I mourned not only the loss to the world but also a relationship that never fully blossomed.

MAKING A DIFFERENCE

Considering Santi's offer, I convinced myself that I could do far more good by learning herbal medicine than I could by returning to Buyat Bay. I also rationalized that living in Kamanta provided far greater opportunity to my bright and inquisitive little Amri than he would ever have in his native village. Still, I could not bring myself to tell Santi the truth about who I was and how I came to live on the island of Sulawesi. Instead, with Santi's help, I wrote a long letter to the people of Buyat Bay trying to convey my decision to remain in Manado to learn herbal medicine, promising to take good care of Amri, and profusely thanking them for what they did for me in my time of need. I ended by saying I hoped they would understand and suggesting that my new skills might one day help them and their children. I assured them that I would one day see them again and return their kindness. Santi arranged for the letter to be brought to the village by a local Dutchman headed to Buyat Bay when he heard of the potential for gold mining. I do not know if they received my letter. I can only hope that they did.

Once the decision was made to remain with Santi, I immersed myself in learning everything he knew about herbal medicine. From ginger tea for curing the common cold to the use of turmeric for easing the pain of arthritis, I realized how much I missed learning new things! Each morning Santi and I would go into the garden to tend to plants such as valerian, mugwort, and wolfberry. When a plant was ready to be harvested we would dry it or boil it, depending on its usage. Santi had small bottles into which the herbs would be placed and labeled for when they were needed.

Working side-by-side with Santi provided me with a new found sense of purpose. He would patiently explain to me which herbs could be combined to address different maladies and which ones should not be combined. He showed me how to measure just the right amounts so as not to create mixtures that were too potent or not potent enough. As instructed, I would taste each one so that I could differentiate them in the event I was presented with a potion with no label. I was struck by just how much each concoction had a unique taste and purpose. Goldenseal could be detected by its bitter taste and was best used to fight infections. Luo han guo, on the other hand, was sweet and could be used to heal sore throats. Santi showed me an entirely new world of healing methods, and watching him with the townspeople taught me that healing take place not only because of the herbs, but because of the healer's heart as well.

Amri also thrived in this new environment. He attended a local school where he soon became a voracious reader in both English and Indonesian. His teacher praised him for his ability to quickly learn new subjects and his willingness to help other children to learn. Unlike me, he had a knack for delving deeply into whatever was being taught and for retaining even the most inconsequential of facts. Over the dinner table each evening, Amri would repeat what he learned, from addition and subtraction to the names of the twenty-five messenger prophets of the Holy Quran; he was proud to share his knowledge on every subject taught to him.

Santi, Amri, and I became a family – a somewhat unusual family for Indonesia, but a family nonetheless. Santi would bring Amri with him to prayer and taught him the ways of the Muslim faith. I would pre-pare simple meals of vegetables, chicken, rice, and fish, and Amri would practice his English by reading aloud to us each evening by gaslight. Santi shared stories about his children, Budi, a boy and, Arida, a girl. He made us laugh out loud hearing their childish pranks and escapades.

We pictured them in our mind's eye as little children behaving in ways children around the world do. I could tell Santi missed his children, but he was proud of the adults they had grown to be.

Gradually, Santi felt he could finally slow down when the townspeople learned that they could trust me to minister to their medical needs. Some days he and I would work together, other days he would sit with the other men along the river while I provided care to our "patients." Under his tutelage I gained a meaningful craft. How ironic that I was not disciplined enough to complete the coursework required to become a doctor in the U.S., yet here I was providing aid to an entire town of people. I suppose it was consistent with my nature to focus on practical information that could be immediately applied rather than things for which I believed I had no use.

Safe from the War

I was not in Kamanta for even one year when news arrived of the Japanese invasion of Manado, several hundred kilometers to our South. It was January 1942 when the fighting started and tales of the invasion were passed along by those fortunate enough to escape. At first, the Indonesians thought the Japanese would liberate them from Dutch rule, but before long they realized they would simply be another sort of interloper. Those who arrived in our town shared stories of the Japanese atrocities as they confiscated food and property for their own use. We watched helplessly and fearfully as Japanese planes flew over head toward Manado. Having no idea whether the invasion would extend to our town, we continued our lives as normally as possible, receiving only sporadic information.

We knew that the world was at war, but we were blessedly removed from the occupation that lasted three years. I could not help but wonder and worry about my family in the United States. I also wondered if I could come to the aid of my new homeland with my skill in aviation. Knowing that this would surely expose my true identity, and that aviation must have changed in the intervening years, I continued to withhold that information, feeling like a traitor in the midst of my adopted country. For all of the turmoil the invasion caused for so many, our lives as a family remained relatively unchanged.

I made friends with many women of the village. They taught me how to sew and use local wood to make household utensils. In return I ministered to them and their families when they were ill and comforted them when there was a death in the family. I never really had women friends when I lived in the United States. There weren't too many who frequented airplane hangars and landing strips. It was a new experience for me to relish the intimacy of friendship and seek it out in the quiet hours when I was not working or tending to my household chores. I learned the comfort that comes from simply being in the presence of another who wants nothing more than to pass the time chatting about the most inconsequential things. There is peace and contentment in the "sisterliness" of other women that I previously did not know existed. The days passed into months and the months faded into years. There was comfort in knowing each day would be the same as the day before and the day after.

Santi's Passing

Santi died in his sleep on March 7, 1945. I'm convinced he waited until he knew the war was over to be certain Amri and I were safe from harm. Amri went to the mosque to let the men of the town know about his passing. One sent his wife to teach me how to prepare the body for burial consistent with Muslim tradition. As we washed Santi for his final resting place and wrapped him in three white sheets, I cried at the loss of my good friend and mentor. Amri, struggling to hold back his own tears, told me that when the Prophet Muhammed's son died he said it is OK to cry but we must remember that Allah is the one who gives life and takes it away at an appointed time. When did my little boy become so wise? I was proud that he had grown into a young man who was not only smart, but sensitive and kind as well. At ten years old he stoically consoled me in my time of grief.

The men of the Kamanta arrived soon thereafter and transferred Santi's body to a makeshift stretcher for the walk to the courtyard outside the Mosque. Word spread quickly of his passing, and the courtyard overflowed with townspeople who loved and respected their healer and friend. Orchids were placed on his body until they were overflowing on the ground. Prayers were said by all, but only men are allowed to carry the body to the final resting place so I returned home with my women friends. In accordance with Muslim tradition, Amri, as the male closest to the deceased, led the procession to the cemetery. Here he watched the only man he could remember as a father figure lowered into his grave, on is right side facing Mecca, with the Imam reciting the final prayers.

Despite the fact that I was not religious, I observed the usual three-day mourning period – out of respect for both Santi and Amri. With no way to get in touch with Santi's children, I received visitors as Amri prayed. In the Muslim faith, it is believed that when a person dies he leaves behind his earthly possessions, but three things continue to benefit him and those his life touched: the charity he showed, the knowledge he shared, and a righteous child who prays for him. This was indeed what Santi had left behind, and all of us who were fortunate enough to be touched by his grace continue to this day to benefit from his blessings.

The weeks and months following Santi's passing left me feeling more alone than ever. He was more than a mentor to me. Santi was the father I never had. Papa was loving, but he did not provide a steady hand from which I could learn. He instilled in me a sense of adventure, but failed to create a stable home environment. I missed the evening ritual with Amri reading and Santi sharing stories from the past. I missed his sage advice. I missed his mere presence. I questioned the decision to keep my true identity from him. It was not until many months later, when going through some of his papers in search of a particular herbal remedy that I found a yellowed article about the disappearance of Amelia Earhart tucked between the pages. Santi knew who I was, or at least he suspected, and loved me enough not to make it an issue between us. It only made me miss him even more.

Santi left me with a home and a skill that enabled me to survive with little money. The townspeople would trade a butchered chicken or a few eggs for my services. Those that had a few rupiahs would pay me in currency when they could. In the back of the house I had a small garden for growing herbs for the remedies and vegetables that I would barter for a pair of pants for Amri or other small household essentials. Our needs were simple. I made every effort to save the rupiah for Amri's future. I wanted him to go to college and live a rich life filled with interesting people and places. I could now understand my father a bit more. His wish that his children have experiences rather than "things" was not dissimilar from what I wished for Amri.

Several months after Santi passed away a young woman no more than seventeen years old whom I recognized from seeing in town knocked at our door. Amri answered and she asked to speak with me about the possibility of becoming our servant. Now you must understand that most Indonesians have servants who live with them to perform routine tasks such as cleaning, cooking, and guarding the house when the occupants are away. They are typically given a room and meals and paid only a few rupiah each month. If they are fortunate, their employers treat them kindly and with respect, but many more are treated no better than slaves. Citra had been the servant of a family who had recently moved away and was left with nowhere to live.

I looked at Amri to gauge his reaction to having someone join our household. He was quick to point out that we had a small room in the back of the house that was being used only for storage. He was a warm-hearted boy always willing to help those less fortunate than himself. After explaining that I could not pay her but would be willing to give her the room in exchange for her services, she eagerly accepted the offer. I showed her the room and said if it suited her we would help her to remove the items being stored and clean it up so that it was habitable. Within hours Citra was situated in her new home, and she quickly went to work preparing our evening meal. As it turned out, she was quite a good cook. Amri devoured her meals like a boy who had not eaten in days. I could not blame him after eating my cooking!

Given that ours was a small home and family, there was little for Citra to do around the house, so I put her to work as my assistant, in much the same way Santi had done for me. Although she had no formal education, she was a quick learner and her personality was well-suited to calming anxious patients. Over time, she learned what each of the herbs was used for and how to combine them for specific remedies. Just as I did with Santi, Citra accompanied me to the garden each morning. But she could speak no English, and I knew without it she would always be limited in terms of what she could make of her life. So each evening Amri and I would take turns tutoring her and gradually she acquired a working knowledge of the language. No longer did she say *selamat pagi* in the morning but rather "good morning." And *terimah kasih* was replaced with "thank you." Before long she could say entire sentences in halting, but grammatically correct English.

Truth be told, I liked having Citra in the house more than I imagined I might. Not because of the housekeeping services she provided, but because I liked teaching others. It was something I missed after leaving Buyat Bay. And in Citra I had a more than willing student. Amri also enjoyed her presence. They teased one another mercilessly as might a brother and sister. I'm sure having someone closer to his own age was a welcome relief from spending so much time alone with middle-aged woman.

We still missed Santi terribly, but together the three of us created yet another family with new rituals and a new routine. I think about the many families I have been fortunate to be part of. I cannot say one was better than the other, but each taught me the importance of not only giving love unconditionally, but accepting it as well. I had grown up with the notion that a family consisted of a mother, father, siblings, grandparents, and aunts and uncles. Love transcends biology, culture, color, and language.

BUDI AND ARIDA

A s 1945 was about to come to a close, a man and woman appeared at the door of our home late one afternoon. They were Indonesian but well dressed in Western style clothing, unlike those of us who lived in Kamanta. The man wore dark trousers and a short-sleeved light blue shirt with an open neck. The woman had on a pink skirt and a white silk blouse that tucked neatly into the waistband. Both sported leather shoes rather than the usual sandals worn by the villagers. Based on their apparent health, I surmised they were not in need of medical attention. The old fear of being exposed rushed through my body. Could they be searching for Amelia Earhart? Hoping they would not notice my heart beating out of my chest, I asked, "Apa yang bias saya bantu?" They seemed perplexed at my asking how I could help them, using my best Indonesian so as not to sound like a Westerner. They said they were looking for their father who lives in this house. These were Santi's children – Arida and Budi! I didn't know whether to hug them or be fearful of them.

The pair appeared to be in their late forties or early fifties. For some reason they existed in my mind's eye as young children. The stories of their childhood antics caused me to memorialize them in their youth. Of course they would not be young, I chastised myself, Santi was over 80 years old when he died. Apologizing for my rudeness, I invited them in and motioned them to please sit. While Citra prepared tea for us they looked around the room politely, taking in the changes since they had last visited. Placing the tea and cups before us, Citra then quietly left the room so that I would have the privacy to share the sad and shocking news that their father had passed away.

Arida immediately began to weep, tears streaming down her face. Budi looked down at his feet, struggling to maintain his composure. He was a taller, more handsome version of his father with short dark hair tinged with gray around the temples. When he moved closer to Arida, putting his arm around her to offer comfort, I could see that he inherited his father's kindness. We sat together in silence for several minutes. When Budi finally spoke, I could hear in his voice the same calm cadence as that of his father. Drawing in a deep breath, he asked who we were and what had happened to Santi.

Realizing that it must have seemed odd to them to see this strange woman living in the home they once shared with their mother and father, I carefully explained how I came to meet Santi and that he generously passed on his knowledge to me hoping that I would continue to care for the people of Kamanta. They asked a few questions pertaining to his death and where he was buried. Arida wanted to be certain her father did not die in pain, Budi wanted to know if he had been in bad health for a period of time. They seemed relieved when I assured them that their father died peacefully in his sleep.

Together we walked to the cemetery and I stood back as they approached the grave marked only with a large stone that Amri and I had placed there soon after the burial. Despite the fact that it was not in Muslim tradition to decorate the gravesite, I nonetheless placed fresh flowers at the site each week. Budi lowered his head in prayer. Arida took his hand in one of hers and wiped her eyes with her other hand. Silently I walked a few meters away so that they could grieve in private. I could hear Budi saying a prayer with his eyes closed and head down. When they were ready to leave, we walked in silence back to the home in which they had been raised. I selfishly wondered if they would ask me to leave. It was, after all, *their* home.

Amri was now home from school. Citra had already filled him in on the visitors who had come from Jakarta. I could tell from the worried look on his face that he too was concerned about what their appearance might mean for us. After introducing him to Arida and Budi I invited them to stay for dinner and the night if they liked. They seemed grateful to be able to remain in the comfort of their childhood home.

The tables were now turned. Whereas Santi used to entertain us over dinner with stories about his children, Arida and Budi now shared stories about Santi. I was fascinated to hear what it was like growing up with Santi. They described him as a loving but also strict father. Budi talked about the time when Santi caught him smoking a clove cigarette. He said his father didn't have to say one word. The look of disappointment on his face was one he would never forget. Arida reminisced about the boys who would meet her around the corner thinking her father didn't know about it, only to later be punished for going out without his permission. Amri listened and laughed as the pair shared their father's reactions to their other childhood exploits, some of which we had already heard from Santi.

With embarrassment over not seeing their father for so long they explained that the war had prevented them from coming to visit sooner. I learned that Arida had never married, opting for a career as a nurse instead. Budi had been married but his wife died in a car accident before they could have children. He worked in finance for the British company, Anglo Indonesia Plantation, Ltd., in Subang, a town south of the capital of Jakarta. Despite the fact that Budi and Arida were slightly older than I, they were Santi's children and I treated them as I would want Amri to be treated by my family should he ever meet them. That evening I made sure Budi and Arida had their old rooms in which to rest. Amri left to stay with a friend and I took the couch. It was a long and emotional day for us all.

Arida had to return to Jakarta the next day. Budi had more flexibility and decided to stay longer. Borrowing a horse and cart from one of the men at the mosque, he took his sister to the small airport just north of town. He asked if I wanted to ride along, but I could not risk being recognized at the air strip. Although my disappearance was likely long forgotten, it was not a chance I wished to take.

After Santi's absence, I was happy to have Budi in the house. It wasn't the presence of a man per se that I appreciated or needed, it was the presence of Santi's flesh and blood that mattered to me. It was the closest thing possible to having Santi near me. He was nearly my own age and his education and worldliness made me feel that I had a peer for the first time in many years. Amri, however, was happy to have another man in a house where he was outnumbered by women. Budi spent his time visiting with old childhood friends and any of their parents who were still alive and helped to repair some things that I could not fix myself.

During the day Citra, and I would tend to the people who came for medical assistance, and in the evenings Budi and I would sit and talk about what was happening in the world. I interrogated him about what he knew about the United States, their involvement in the war, and how President and Mrs. Roosevelt were doing. I was saddened to learn that the President had died shortly after being inaugurated for an unprecedented fourth term the year before. I silently wondered how my friend Eleanor was doing without her husband.

It was even more shocking was to learn about Adolph Hitler and the horrors that took place in German concentration camps. I could not imagine why anyone would want to exterminate an entire race of people. Budi told me about the Dutch occupation of Indonesia and how the associated atrocities, although not on the scale of Nazi Germany, devastated entire families and villages. I shared with him the summer day in Toronto when I saw four one-legged men struggling to navigate their way down the street on crutches. It was the first time I was touched so personally and closely by war.

I told Budi how I immediately quit the Ogontz School, registered for a first-aid course, joined the Military Aid Detachment, and was assigned to Canada's Spadina Military Hospital. I simply could not go back to high school knowing there were people who needed my help. From that time on I had no patience with talk of war or the military. So many young lives were needlessly wasted because men cannot resolve their differences humanely. I often wonder what the world would be like if only it was run by women and not men hell bent on war.

Budi showed an interest in me and my background, but I only guardedly shared information about growing up in the United States, my family, and my own education. When he asked how I came to be a missionary I changed the subject by asking if he would like some tea, and in true Indonesian fashion he was too polite to press the issue. We had only met a few days before, yet we shared so many intimacies in a short time that I felt I knew him for my entire life. I was surprised at my disappointment when he brought up the subject of leaving.

The night before Budi was to leave, he asked whether Amri and I would like to accompany him back to Subang. I could not fathom leaving Kamanta and my work, and I was not willing to risk being recognized and forced to return to the chaotic existence I once called my life. As much as I would miss Budi, I could not do it. He did not press me but did promise to return in the near future and assured me that Amri and I could remain in Santi's home for as long as we chose. With that, I breathed a sigh of relief.

RETURN TO BUYAT BAY

The house seemed oddly empty without Budi. It was 1950 now and I had lived there for over three years without him and one week suddenly seemed like a lifetime. Amri, approaching his teen years, talked about Budi like one would talk about a big brother – despite the immense difference in their ages. He missed Budi even more than I did and mentioned him constantly--"Budi said" I should study this or "Budi said" I should pray that way. Sharing their spiritual beliefs was good for Amri. I could be a good role model for him in terms of living a spiritual life but could not help him on his Muslim journey. I believe there is a God but not the God worshipped in so many religions. To me God is a powerful presence that guides my actions and helps me to be a better person. He (or she!) is not a punitive or directive spirit that dictates what those actions should be.

The months that passed after Arida's and Budi's visit were the loneliest ones I experienced since my rescue. How odd that their visit made me yearn for something I had not had for nearly a decade. Perhaps because they were part of Santi I wanted them to be part of my life. I could see in them his actions and words, and it made me miss him all the more. Each knock on the door raised my hopes that it might just be them returning to see us, and each time I was disappointed. With no phones and no post, there was no way to contact them, even if I thought it might be remotely appropriate to do so.

As the Republic of Indonesia was in its infancy, the long arm of government reached into all aspects of the people's lives. Sukarno became the first president and councils were formed at local levels. Roads, education, and sanitary conditions all improved. Work crews began paving a road to what were now actively developed mines in Buyat Bay. Rickety buses were available for transport. My wandering spirit longed to return to visit my earliest Indonesian friends, and I wanted Amri to reconnect with his past. When he finished school in June of 1946 he and I traveled by bus to Buyat Bay. By then Citra had learned enough to be able assist patients with rudimentary ailments, so she remained behind to watch the so-called shop.

Riding the bus in the daytime, I could see what a treacherous (and foolish) journey I had made alone by Jeep. Amri was bored with the monotonous travel, seeing nothing but jungle for kilometers on end. Of course he had no memory of our original trip on this road. When we finally arrived at Buyat Bay I found it to be unrecognizable. As a result of the mining development, it had transitioned from a village to a town. The huts in which we once resided were replaced with houses much the same as the one in which we now lived in Kamanta. Most of the trees had been cut down, and the rice paddy was nowhere to be seen. Heavy equipment on the edge of town hauled ore out of the mines. The fishermen were enlisted to work the mines, and what I once thought of as an idyllic existence was polluted with the by-product of industrialization.

After the six-hour bus trip, Amri and I were dirty and tired. We had anticipated finding things as we left them, but, just as we had changed, so had the village and its people. It was far from familiar and difficult to get my bearings without the old familiar markers. We looked for anyone we might know who would offer us their hospitality. After walking several blocks past pushcarts filled with fruits and vegetables, we finally saw a woman who recognized us. Our eyes met at the same time, and Etty ran up to hug first me then, after careful inspection and recognizing him as a grown-up version of the child she once knew, Amri. She invited us to her home where we exchanged stories of the years that had passed. We gratefully accepted her offer to stay at her house.

Etty walked me through the town, stopping now and then to re-introduce me to members of the village who once cared for me so lovingly. Each was warm in their greeting, yet at the same time gone was the innocence that once characterized the essence of who they were. The joyful abandon with which they once went about their work and play had disappeared. It was replaced with a weariness that is borne of being robbed of your culture and values.

Children returned from working in the mines, covered with soot and with vacant looks in their eyes. Even after being reminded that I was the woman who would sing to them and teach them English, they were too tired to respond. Sadly, the ones who had shown promise in the school I had started were no longer able to speak English. I felt an immense sense of guilt. Perhaps if I had returned to the village I could have prevented this from happening. There are always so many choice points in one's life. I could regret every choice I made if I gave it enough thought. But seeing the eyes that looked out from empty souls of these once vibrant, care-free children haunts me to this day. I saved one child at the expense of so many others. For that I could never forgive myself.

Amri and I spent several days becoming reacquainted with our former family members, only to learn we no longer had anything in common. Education was nonexistent. The sense of community in which we once lived and thrived had disappeared. It was a sad reminder of what happens when one chooses one life over another. If I no longer had anything in common with these people, what would it be like if I returned to the United States? Surely I would have even less in common with my old friends and family. If ever I thought of returning to that life, this experience caused me to seriously question the wisdom of such a move.

GRATEFUL

After nearly a week in Buyat Bay, Amri and I gave our thanks to Etty and returned home tired and disillusioned. The anticipation we felt when starting our journey was soon doused when we realized the negative impact the developers had on the village and its people. Amri was now anxious to return to his friends. I was anxious to return to my work. I wondered if he thought about the fact that it very well could have been him working in those mines. His silence combined with staring out the window of the bus on the ride home led me to believe he knew how fortunate he was. When I reached over and took his hand he squeezed so tightly that I thought my fingers would break. I knew my boy. That was his way of saying thank you.

How often does this happen when we return to the community we once knew? We change, but those who remain behind do not change in the same direction with us. For many weeks after our visit I continued to chastise myself for not returning. I believed my presence could have made a difference in the lives of those who remained behind. But the reality is, progress (if that's what you would call what happened in Buyat Bay) whether planned and purposeful or not, happens despite our best efforts. Had I remained, Amri and I might also have become casualties of the change experienced by those in Buyat Bay.

Reaching the front door to the house, we were surprised and delighted to find Budi sitting on the couch talking to Citra. Amri ran into his arms and Budi responded with a long, warm hug. I think I was too tired to do anything but smile. Secretly, I was overjoyed to see him.

I do not know what makes it so difficult for me to express my deepest emotions. Even as a child I was more stoic than emotional. Perhaps having grown up around parents who themselves acted out of emotion rather than with deliberate objectivity required me to be the adult in most situations. Only in the sky was I released from the weight of my sober existence.

That evening flew by as we traded stories about what had happened in the intervening months. Budi was promoted. I concocted a new herbal remedy for arthritis. Amri had read *Great Expectations*. And Citra was ever more fluent in English. The most trivial of events took on a new significance. Budi brought a chess game with him and began the process of teaching Amri how to play as Citra and I went about making dinner for the four of us. Amri went to bed that night tired but elated that Budi had returned to him. I sometimes forgot that Amri's earliest attachments had ended before he could comprehend why. The few courses in psychology that I had taken years ago taught me that these connections form the foundation of our ability to build lasting relationships later in life. The loss of both his mother and father had surely affected Amri in ways I would never be able to totally comprehend. As much as he loved me, and I know he did, I was not Indonesian. We did not share a collective unconscious in the way he and Budi did.

Despite my fatigue, Budi and I stayed up late into the night sharing the minutest details of our lives since we had last seen one another. When I said it was time for me to go to bed, Budi stood and looked at me with eyes so penetrating that it took my breath away. I stood still as he walked toward me, encircling his arms around me. It had been so long since I felt the tender touch of another adult human being. It did not feel the same as G.P.'s hugs, which even after all this time I could recall but not describe as tender. No, being held by Budi was like being embraced by the limbs of a towering oak tree. Strong and steady. For the first time since Grandpa Otis held me after a fall from the swing in our back yard I felt an overwhelming sense of being safe and protected.

It was on this night and with that embrace that my relationship with Budi moved from the closest of friendships to lovers. Sensing my hesitation Budi stepped back, but his eyes never left mine. Finally, after what seemed like an eternity, I took his hand and led him into my bedroom. We undressed and climbed into bed hungry for each other's touch. Gently he made love to me. He was a considerate and tender lover. He did nothing without first looking into my eyes for approval. It was as if we had done this hundreds of times before, yet with the newness and excitement of a first time. We fell asleep in one another's arms knowing that our lives had been forever changed.

A Companion for Life

After so many years living alone, or at least without the intimate companionship of a man, Budi made me long for something I had never had – something I never believed was even possible. Before G.P. there had been other suitors in my life, but instinctively I knew they were not the right men for me. My fierce independence required a maturity typically missing in young men, or most men for that matter. Long ago I had given up the belief that I would ever find a true partner who saw who I was and unconditionally accepted me. In my wildest imagination I never believed I would find such love at this stage of my life. It filled me with both joy for the gift that had been given to me and fear over the thought of being unworthy of it.

Budi proved to be everything I could possibly want in a friend and a lover. Unlike G.P., he was gentle and caring. He wanted from me only what I was willing to give and nothing more. He did not try to push me in this direction or pull me toward that one as G.P. so often did. Budi was more apt to observe and follow my lead, or at least ask what I wanted, rather than expect me to blindly follow him.

At first we attempted to hide the depth of our relationship from Amri. Neither of us knew for certain where the relationship would take us, and we did not want to create false expectations, disappoint him, or create unnecessary turmoil in his life. But as a sensitive and caring young man, Amri sensed the change. He became more protective of me, not wanting to leave Budi and me alone for even an hour. He became belligerent with Budi, refusing to do as asked and holding his ground with rebellion. I had no experience in how to handle this shift in his behavior but was concerned about the escalating tension in the house between the three of us. I would not want to be in the position of having to make a choice between Amri and Budi, but if I had to choose one there was no question it would be my boy.

One day while Citra and I were busy tending to an old woman who had come for treatment, I heard Budi invite Amri out for a walk. When they returned, Amri was a different child. Apparently Budi had convinced him that nothing could ever interfere with the love I felt for Amri. I do not know all that they discussed, but with a barely imperceptible difference Amri began relating to Budi as a father, not a brother. Slowly Amri began to accept the relationship between Budi and me. As he returned to his usual self, we once again shared wonderful evenings when he showed off his prowess in English by reading aloud the most difficult passages of books by Mark Twain and Ernest Hemingway.

Budi no longer slept in his boyhood room but with me in the room that once belonged to this mother and father. Our lovemaking was filled with tenderness and the closest thing I could describe as bliss. Comparing it with the time I spent with G.P., I now realize I was simply another possession for G.P., a man-boy spoiled by privilege and power. I'm certain he loved me in his way, but that was just the problem. It was always his way. How prescient I was to write him that note the evening before our wedding informing him that we should both consider this marriage a trial. I would not even assume his last name – something unheard of in 1931 – when we hastily wed at his mother's home in Connecticut.

The truth was, ours was a marriage of convenience. G.P. needed an enterprise to distinguish himself from his publishing family, and I needed to find a way to financially support my family – and myself for that matter. I had hoped over time we would come to love one another in a different way, but it gradually became clear that this was unlikely. I cannot say I am sorry that I married G.P. If not for him my family would surely have struggled financially. As long as Mother and Muriel followed the instructions I left with G.P. and my attorney, they would be provided for. Ironically, if not for him I would not have the life I now live and love. I suppose that it's a sad truism of life that only in making the difficult choice to leave behind what we do not want can we find what we do want and need.

FAILING HEALTH

It has been nearly one month since I've written anything about my life. My stay in the hospital was longer than originally anticipated. The cancer has spread, and although the prognosis is not good I am prepared to meet my fate in due time. I have lived a full and long life filled with more good than bad, more love than sadness, and enough adventure for two (or three!) lifetimes. My only hope is that I have enough time and energy to complete my story so that the mystery can once and for all be put to rest. Why just the other day I saw yet another article in the newspaper declaring someone had found the remains of Amelia Earhart. Little do they know she is quite alive, if not well. But I cannot complain. I am surrounded by love.

Yet Another Family

I fondly remember the years after WWII as the best of my entire life. Budi, Amri, Citra, and I became a family, albeit an unusual one for the place and time. Budi continued to live in Subang, coming to visit us whenever he could. During each visit, he asked me to marry him and return to Subang with him so that he, Amri, and I could live as a more traditional family. I know he struggled with the religious aspect of our relationship as it now stood, but how could I marry him before I revealed who I really was? Budi – and everyone else for that matter – continued to know me as just Meely, a Christian missionary turned herbal healer.

As much as I missed Budi during the long periods we lived apart, my focus on raising Amri, providing Citra with a trade that she could depend on throughout her life, and healing all those who walked through my door were of great importance to me. In some ways it felt like the penance I had to pay for deserting my family, the villagers of Buyat Bay, and deceiving the rest of the world. Budi did not press me, but always made it clear that he was ready to marry whenever I was. He knew I loved him with all my heart. I just could not risk being identified as someone other than Meely.

By then, nearly thirteen years after my rescue by the kind fishermen of Buyat Bay, I do not know whether I would have even been recognizable. My hair was long and no longer blonde but white. My former fair complexion of Northern European ancestry had been replaced by a leathered, rugged look from years spent in the sun. My once delicate hands were wrinkled and stained beyond repair from mixing herbs into teas. And I was no longer the skinny string bean of my youth. I had filled out in the ways that women do as they get older. Looking in the mirror, I wasn't sure even I would have recognized the reflection as being that of Amelia Earhart!

I do not know how years passed one into the next with nothing worthy of discussion taking place, but they did. That is not to say the years were not full or rewarding for they were. If not for Amri growing taller and more manly with each passing month, I do not know whether I would have marked the passing of the years at all. How luxurious to finally live a "normal" life after a childhood and young adulthood filled with such drama. And is this not how most people live their lives? As Henry David Thoreau wrote in Walden, most men live lives of quiet desperation. My life may be quiet in comparison with the years spent in the public eye, but I am far from desperate.

The turning point came when Amri turned 18. It was time for him to attend university – he was far too bright to remain in our little town. Budi and I discussed it when he came in February of that year and it was agreed that Amri would enroll in the Bandung University of Technology. It was time to make a difficult decision. Do I let Amri leave by himself to live with and be taken care of by Budi, or do I go with them so that we may once and for all live together as a family?

I struggled mightily with the decision. I no longer thought of myself as Amelia Earhart. She was a person I knew long ago. I resembled her neither physically nor in spirit. What difference would it make if I continued as Meely? Then I realized that starting our life together with a lie would not be fair to Budi. He deserved to know the truth. It was better that he learned it from me than from someone trying to capitalize on solving the mystery of Amelia Earhart. If he were to reject me because I had lied all of these years, it was better to know before giving up my life in Kamanta. And if by some miracle he chose to continue to love me despite my deceit I would need his support in continuing to live anonymously. Of course there was always the risk that he would knowingly or otherwise reveal my presence to others, thereby making it impossible to continue with my current existence, but that was a risk I had to consider taking.

Unburdening a Lie

One day when Amri went out to play football with his friends, Budi and I took a walk in the meadow at the edge of town. I cannot recall the exact words I used but I told Budi that I was not the person he thought me to be. He never stopped walking or holding my hand, he simply listened. Baring my soul, I explained first about landing the Electra at sea, Noonan's death, being rescued by the fishermen, and finally telling him my true name. When I finished my story we continued walking hand-in-hand in silence for what seemed like an eternity. Finally, Budi walked us toward a large banyan tree and indicated he wanted us to sit beneath it. I could not imagine what he was thinking for he gave no clue until he spoke, and those words I do recall as if they were said just yesterday.

"You are my Meely. You will always be my Meely. I will protect you and keep you safe from harm. I do not love you for your name or because of your past. I love you because of who you are today. Who you are with me. Who you are to Amri." Then he revealed a secret of his own. Budi had known my identity all along. By coincidence or fate, I believe the latter, he was in Bandung thirteen years earlier when the Electra landed for repairs and was delayed by a monsoon. One day during our stay in the town, Noonan and I took a tour of a nearby inactive volcano. Budi was there with a guest from his company's London office, also visiting the volcano. He couldn't help but notice the Americans and their entourage and, after inquiring who we were, learned it was Amelia Earhart and Fred Noonan.

Upon meeting me the first time during his visit to Kamanta with his sister Arida (when they learned of their father's passing), he thought I looked familiar but could not place where he might have seen me. When he returned to Subang he contacted the Christian Mission office in Jakarta to inquire about a missionary by the name of Meely. They informed him that they had no record of such a missionary. The thought of an imposter living in his father's home disturbed him. It weighed heavily on his mind until one day he was jolted by a memory tucked deep into the recesses of his mind of that trip to the volcano. Traveling to Bandung, he searched the university library for information about Amelia Earhart. He came upon a picture of Noonan and me standing in a hangar with several Indonesian mechanics. Although I looked different, he was convinced that I was the missing aviator. He made a copy of the picture and kept it in his wallet. Pulling it out now he explained that as we shared more information about our pasts, his suspicions were confirmed. My stories about growing up in Kansas with a sister named Muriel and attending school in Canada were part of the historical record. I still have that picture.

Listening to him, I heaved a deep sigh that expelled more than a decade of pent-up fear. I felt my body relax in a way I do not think it had for so many years. Keeping up the invisible shield to hide my real identify had taken more energy than I realized. I no longer worried about being discovered. I knew that Budi would protect me from whatever might ensue. Together we would face the future with no secrets between us. Hearing my sigh he leaned over and kissed me, then wrapped his arms tightly around me. I buried my head in his chest and cried. I'd kept the secret for so long and after revealing it to this person whom I treasured so, I once again learned and felt what it meant to be loved unconditionally. All along he loved me enough to keep my secret from others, accept me for who I had become, and patiently wait for me to share the truth. And for all of these reasons and more, I wanted to spend the rest of my life with him.

LEAVING HOME AGAIN

In the summer of 1952, Budi, Amri, and I carefully packed the contents of our home in Kamanta – the home in which Budi had been born, the only home that Amri remembered, and the home that had protected and sheltered me for so many years. We had invited Cinta to join us, but by now she was quite a proficient herbal medicine practitioner in her own right and wanted to remain in Kamanta to continue the work begun by Santi. I was so proud of the woman she had become. She was dating a young man from the village who had his own woodworking shop. I could see whenever they were together that they shared a deep affection and imagined that one day they would marry.

When the horse-drawn cart appeared at the door, Budi and Amri loaded it with our few belongings. Budi suggested that I not take the herbs with me as they would be even more readily available in Subang. I went from house to house bidding farewell to my dear friends and patients. I knew I would not see them again. Leaving Kamanta and these people was bittersweet. When it came time to say good-bye to Cinta we clung tightly to one another until Budi gently touched my shoulder, an indication that it was time to go. Now I knew what I meant to Santi, for Cinta was more than just a protégé, she was a beloved member of my ever expanding family. "Sempai jumpa lagi, temen saya." *Until next time we see one another, my friend.*

The journey to Subang was as exciting as any airplane trip I had ever flown. The cart took our belongings and the three of us to a train that would bring us to the port in Donggala. From there, we boarded the boat that would take us to Jakarta. We planned on staying a few days with Arida in Jakarta before heading South by train to our final destination of Subang.

I was surprised at how being on a boat for the first time since my rescue brought back such a flood of strong memories and emotions. As the shore disappeared from view and we sailed the choppy waters of the Makkasar Sea, I found myself re-living the days spent floating with Noonan in the Pacific Ocean wondering whether we would be rescued or instead die at sea. In my mind's eye, I saw Noonan gradually slipping beneath the surface of the water as I watched helplessly. Involuntarily my body shuddered. Sensing something wrong, Budi silently put his around me. Having told him all I could remember from my trauma at sea, he instinctively knew the trip would be difficult for me and stayed close without intruding on my private thoughts.

Budi and Amri spent the time at sea reading, playing chess, and talking about what university would be like in September. I reveled in watching the two most important men in my life huddled with their heads together looking every bit the part of father and son. We were at sea for three days before Amri ran breathlessly up to the deck where I was reading, pointing to our first glimpse of shore. Little did he know how much his life was about to change. The little boy had grown to become a fine man, and the man was about to become a citizen of the world.

After living in small villages for over a decade, the bustling port of Jakarta was an assault on my senses. Between the noisy blaring of the ship's horns and the shouting of the men working at the dock, I wanted to make a hasty retreat back to Kamanta. I had to keep reminding myself that this was simply a new adventure. Surely Budi did not live with this kind of chaos in his life. Sensing how overwhelmed I was, Budi once again appeared by my side and we stood together with Amri watching the sailors tie the boat up in port.

Seeing a Western woman with two Indonesian men was quite a curiosity in those days. It was much more common to see a Dutchman with an Asian wife. At first I was uncomfortable with the stares we received, but that discomfort was minimal compared with the ever-present fear of being discovered. How long would this fear nag at me? Now that we were among city people someone would no doubt recognize me. Although I knew I looked nothing like the woman in the pictures from over a decade ago, I wore a straw hat with a large brim that covered the top half of my face and kept my head down as we disembarked the boat.

Amri, on the other hand, was wide eyed with amazement. He had never seen so much commotion and industry. He could not believe the crowds in the streets and the number of warungs (small shops) lined up one after another. To be truthful, even I was in awe of all the cars and thousands of people. I never imagined that Jakarta would be so modern with electric trolleys zipping through the narrow streets. Wires criss-crossed the skies above the city, allowing the trolleys to operate in all sectors of the city. Becak – pedaling bicycles – outnumbered the cars. I felt as if I had returned to San Francisco – at least this was the way I remembered it when I departed.

JAKARTA

We made our way to Arida's house in Jakarta. It was a home formerly occupied by the Dutch and therefore European in style and much more modern than our home in Kamanta – and a far cry from my hut in Buyat Bay! Upon our arrival, Arida was not home but recognizing Budi, her servant allowed us to gain admittance. Amri and I were in wonder with the luxurious amount of space available compared with the modest home we left behind. There were four bedrooms, a bathroom with indoor plumbing, a living room, dining room, small kitchen, and, off of that was a tiny room, a cubbyhole really, where the servant stayed. The large bathtub was not lost on me, and soon I was immersed in warm water that cleansed me of the grime, anticipation, and anxiety that had accumulated during our sea voyage.

Although Arida did not anticipate our arrival on this particular day, she did not let on that she was in the least surprised when she arrived home from her work as a nurse at Gatot Soebroto Army Hospital. She went out of her way to make us feel welcome and at ease in our new surroundings. Clearly Budi had discussed our relationship with her, and I wondered whether her Muslim upbringing would cause her to be uncomfortable with us. But she showed no sign of judgment, showing us to the bedroom that we would share despite the fact that we were not married.

Of course Budi was already comfortable, but Amri and I were like country bumpkins in awe of the deluxe surroundings. When dinner time came, it was difficult to pull Amri away from the window where he watched the flurry of activity on the street. Arida's servant made us a delicious dinner of nasi goreng with fried chicken, and we all sat down together to enjoy the food that was prepared for us as if it were the most usual of occasions. Looking around the dinner table at my new family, I was filled with both gratitude and sorrow. I recalled family dinners with my mother, father, grandparents, and Muriel and I seated together, chatting up a storm about what happened that day or was about to happen the next. Here in Jakarta was the closest I had come to resurrecting the kind of family I had known in the United States. Another bittersweet moment.

After dinner, Arida encouraged Amri to walk around the neighborhood as the adults talked about the future. At first I was afraid to allow Amri to explore on his own, but Arida and Budi assured me that it was safe and no harm would come to him. Reluctantly I agreed that he could spend an hour on his own, making him promise to return as soon as it became dark. I can now admit that I worried about him every time he ventured out on his own, and this evening was no different.

I was surprised to find that Arida also knew my true identify. I suppose I should have realized that Budi would confide in his sister, but it had not occurred to me until this point. It was a pleasant realization that she would do anything possible to maintain my anonymity so that her brother could be happy. She had done research at the Jakarta library and found articles about my disappearance. She pushed a pile of papers and books toward me and suggested I look at them when I was ready. She then politely asked if she could ask me questions about my previous life.

I was torn. It had been so many years since I was Amelia Earhart and presently wanted nothing more than to be Meely the Christian missionary turned wife and mother. But I knew that to gain Arida's trust I had to allow her to explore my past. It is in letting people see us for who we really are that we forge unbreakable bonds. Until then, a relationship is simply built on sand. So after I nodded assent, we talked for almost an hour about how I came to arrive in Buyat Bay, my journey to Kamanta, and my relationship with Amri.

Arida was not overtly doubting my story, but it was clear that she did want to verify who I was. I could not blame her for being protective of her beloved brother. I envied how they cared for one another in this very special way. After I answered her myriad questions she seemed satisfied that I was indeed who I claimed to be and shifted her inquiry to what Budi and I would be doing in the future. All discussion of Amelia Earhart ceased once Amri returned to the house breathlessly describing what he just experienced.

One Last Move

After spending three days in Jakarta, Budi, Amri, and I said our good-byes to Arida and boarded a bus for Subang. During our time in Jakarta, I had the opportunity to buy fabrics to sew clothing and purchase household items as well as Chinese herbs from a store front with a sign that read "Toko Obat Tjina Merk Tje Ann." The shop was owned by a Chinese woman named Ann. Although she regarded me with initial skepticism, she eventually shared some of her formulas for common ailments such as diarrhea, arthritis, and typhus. Both the advice and the herbs would be needed to get started as a healer in my soon to be new home.

As much as I enjoyed our few days in the city, I was anxious to return to the peacefulness of the country. I also did not want to live with the ever-present fear of being discovered, which was never far from my mind when I walked the streets of Jakarta with my floppy hat and head down. If ever I harbored thoughts of returning to Los Angeles, they were dashed once and for all after spending time in Jakarta. The city was filled with wonder, but I was no longer interested in the hustle and bustle. Living a simple life was so much more satisfying and fulfilling than any aspect of my previous life – but for one, and that of course was flying. I still missed the feeling of exhilaration that came as my plane climbed into the clouds to the steady humming of the plane. It was, in fact, is big price to pay for living life on my own terms. Whereas I had always believed that having everything I could possibly want was within my grasp, I now realized that life is more often a series of trade-offs. Flying is an expensive proposition. To be able to do so required me to endorse products and attend events that I would rather not have had to. Living anonymously meant that I would most likely never again pilot an airplane. How ironic that what brought me to my new life could never be a part of my future. I long ago reconciled, however, that living fully and freely is a different kind of freedom than being in the air but is freedom nonetheless. It is the freedom I chose.

The bus ride to Subang looked familiar. In the outskirts of the city, tea plantations, rice fields, and banana groves dominated the landscape. I immediately felt more in my element. The warungs, mosques, and men in traditional Muslim attire made me once again feel at home and safe. We rode for nearly four hours with many stops and starts along the way to allow other passengers to enter and exit the bus before Budi finally indicated that we would disembark at the next stop.

The bus driver, Amri and Budi unloaded our belongings onto the side of the road and the bus took off leaving us in a trail of dust from the dirt road. Budi immediately took charge and spoke with a becak driver who was waiting at the bus stop. Together the men loaded our personal belongings into the cab of the tricycle, and we walked alongside. I would be less than honest if I didn't say I wondered where we were going and what the future held in store for Amri and me, but I trusted Budi and walked silently toward the house I would forever more call home.

It was late afternoon, and the smell of garlic and vegetables cooking wafted from the homes along the way. After walking for not more than ten or fifteen minutes, we came upon a tract of land where there was a two-story house. It was not like the bamboo Indonesian homes to which I had become accustomed. Nor was it as fancy as the European style homes in Jakarta. It was built from mortar and wood with a sturdy roof that appeared to provide adequate protection against the heavy rains. All around the perimeter of the house was a porch that could be accessed by large louvered doors. As the becak driver unloaded our belongings and brought them into the house, a young woman opened the door to greet us. Budi introduced her as his servant, Tuti, and she smiled and bowed as we made our way into our new home.

Subang

The days immediately following our arrival in Subang were the beginning of bliss as I had never before known in my life. Each time I looked into Budi's eyes I felt content in the knowledge that this was the man with whom I would spend the rest of my life. The years of coming together only to have him depart for weeks and sometimes months at a time were finally in the past. We were finally a family. A real family. With a house, stability and individual goals.

I could not help but compare it to the early years of my marriage to G.P. Coming from a large, successful family dominant in the world of book publishing, G.P. maneuvered through the world with the kind of confidence that comes from privilege. Wanting to make his mark on the world separate and apart from his family, I realize that I was merely a conduit to that end. Now that I have experienced the joy of a deep and everlasting intimate bond I know it was not marital love that we shared, but rather a marriage of convenience.

I sometimes think of the things G.P. insisted that I do in the name of raising money for my flights, to purchase a bigger plane, or to simply live the Los Angeles lifestyle to which he was accustomed. I had little interest in advertising appliances or speaking before large groups, but I allowed myself to be convinced these were necessary evils in pursuit of flying. Even our marriage on February 7, 1931, was conducted as a business affair, attended only by a judge (friend of the family) and G.P.'s mother and uncle. Immediately following the Saturday ceremony in Connecticut at his mother's estate, we returned to New York for work on Monday. Perhaps it should have been an omen to which I paid better attention when the *New York Times* announcement described us as "undemonstrative."

Our first order of business was enrolling Amri in Bandung Institute of Technology for the fall semester. Budi took Amri on the train to Bandung for a three-day visit to the city. I stayed behind to get the house in order. Although I was not the best of homemakers, Budi's house needed a woman's touch to truly become a home. Together with Tuti, I sewed simple curtains for the windows, visited with local women who handcrafted rugs and purchased several for the bedrooms and living room, and bought much needed cooking utensils so that I could assist with the preparation of our meals. I appreciated having a servant for those things I did not want to do, but I still wanted to be part of the process of cooking for Budi and Amri.

While they were away in Bandung, I took the opportunity to begin planting an herb garden in the back of the house. The land was fertile and being in the mountains meant there would be plenty of rain to nourish my seedlings. Although she did not have to, Tuti came out to help me, and as we planted I learned more about her impoverished childhood and that she had come to work for Budi when she was just twelve years old. She explained that Budi was kind to her and did not beat her like some of the employers of other servants. Then she glanced at me as if to say, "You won't beat me will you?" Only time would prove to her that I had no desire to do her harm. She had been loyal and honest in Budi's employ, and that was enough to gain my trust.

When Amri and Budi returned from Bandung it seemed to me as if Amri had matured years in just the few days he had been away. Three days was the longest I had ever been separated from him, and to watch him come breathlessly into the house I viewed him with fresh eyes. Animatedly, he provided a detailed account of what had transpired on the trip. He talked about the university, the students he had met who offered to help him acclimate once the semester started, the professors to whom he was introduced by Budi, and where he would be living. As

he spoke, my mind wandered back to the small village of Buyat Bay and the little boy who would climb into my bed so many years ago.

I could not help but think about the many children I left behind on the night I went in search of medical assistance for Amri. I recalled seeing them during our visit years later and how different their lives were from Amri's. It was painful to relive the choices I could have made that might have saved them all from their fates. And isn't this how retrospection often makes one feel? What is the saying? Hindsight is 20/20. I remember a psychology teacher once saying that to truly help others, and ourselves, we must accept that we make decisions for the best possible reasons in the moment. It is only in retrospect that we can determine that there might have been a better choice. The older I become, the more willing I am to forgive myself the choices that were not in the best interests of others. When I made those choices, I felt as though I truly had no other alternatives.

The month before Amri left for school was spent preparing for his departure. The preparation went beyond simply purchasing a trunk to hold his belongings, new clothing, and the items he would need in the apartment he would share with several other boys (young men, I had to remind myself). Although he always showed good judgment and a sense of responsibility, Budi talked to him about what it was like to live on one's own for the first time. He cautioned him to be vigilant about what was happening around him and to choose his friends carefully for they would play a large part in his experience not only at university but in the future as well. At night as we lay in bed, Budi tried to prepare me for the day when Amri would start the next chapter of his life.

I thought I would stoically respond when the time came for Amri to leave for university in October 1950. How foolish I was to think that I could let my boy go without emotion. I struggled to keep my tears at bay. Amri had become a fine young man with a good mind and an even better heart. He hugged me and whispered in my ear, "Do not worry, Meely. I am never far away from you." And with this, welled up emotions broke through the thin barrier of restraint. Tears streamed down my face as I waved good-bye watching Amri and Budi head down the path to the train station. I stood and watched until they turned a corner and I could no longer see them.

Despite the fact that I intellectually knew that our bond would never be broken, we had been through much too much together for that to happen, I intuitively knew it would never be the same. As was appropriate for a young man his age, he was embarking on a new path that would take him to places where I could not join him and where even he could not now imagine.

The house suddenly seemed vacant and silent, but I realized it was my heart that was emptiest. It felt like a piece of my soul had been wrenched away. The days immediately following his departure I went about my daily tasks but with little energy or enthusiasm. Sensing my despair, Tuti stayed closer than usual, trying to comfort me with tea and conversation. I was grateful for her efforts and not wanting to make her feel as if she failed me, I put on a brave face. Alone at night in my bed-room, I gave myself permission to grieve Amri's absence.

When I couldn't sleep, I would steal out of bed and tip-toe into the room Amri had only briefly inhabited. Touching the model mosque he made in school, smelling his jacket, and finally laying down in his bed, I allowed my mind to remember the wonderful years he and I spent together. Even though I had long ago lost everyone and everything that was important to me, this was somehow different. It was as if a piece of the tapestry of my soul that could never be replaced had walked out the door. I could finally vividly experience how those I left behind in the United States must have felt. Although over the years I felt enormous guilt for what I put them through, it was not until now that I could feel it from *their* perspective.

When Budi returned from his trip taking Amri to school, he found me working in the garden – a momentary distraction from the over-whelming feeling of loss. I thought my tears had been spent, but a new flood of heartache washed over me when I saw him. We stood entwined together, Budi holding me closer with each wave of sobs. Once again, Budi's gentle embrace encouraged me to do what I needed to do. Words weren't necessary, nor would they help. Finally I moved away, took his hand and together we walked to the porch, sank into the rocking chairs, and I implored him to tell me every detail of what had happened in the preceding days.

Slowly I regained my sense of self and allowed myself to relish the warm surroundings of my home with Budi. Whereas leaving my family and friends behind in the United States was a choice I made in an effort to live a more fulfilling life, having Amri grow up and start his own life was a natural part of the life cycle but did not serve me in a positive way. Do not misunderstand. I believed it was time for Amri to spread his wings, but it did not make it any less painful. Just remembering this day two decades ago floods me once more with emotion. Cukup hari ini (enough for today).

Letting Go

The months following Amri's departure for university I focused on gaining the trust of the villagers in Subang. I began by visiting with the local shopkeepers, telling them about the herbal remedies that I could offer. I knew in a small village like Subang they would spread the word to their patrons. Each day I would visit a different household, most much more modest than the one I shared with Budi and more like the home we had in Kamanta. Speaking with the residents I encouraged them to visit me when they had a sick child or family member who needed assistance.

At first I was able to use one of the rooms of our home as my "clinic." But as the stream of villagers requiring attention increased, more space was required. Budi arranged for some of the workers from his company to build a separate structure on the land behind our home for this purpose. Although Amri was never far from my mind or heart, the activity consumed my attention. By mid-December of that year, I had a fully operational place within which to work. Tuti would assist me with examinations by entertaining frightened children with puppets she had sewn from scrap cloth. She did not show the same promise as Cinta, but her services were invaluable nonetheless. Another lesson I had learned over the years.

If you expect people to be like you, you will always be disappointed. But if you accept people as they are and appreciate their unique gifts, you will be pleasantly surprised at how much they add to your life. I realize now just how impatient and judgmental I was in my youth. If someone didn't do something fast enough or the way I would do it, it wasn't good enough. I'm mortified to think how badly I must have made people feel.

Budi resumed his own routine of going to his office at Anglo Indonesian Plantation, Ltd., where he was a financial executive for this company that produced tea, rubber, tapioca, chocolate, and rice (this was what entitled him to such a lovely home, originally built by the Dutch owner of the company in the early 1900s). At night over dinner, we would share stories about our respective days. Sometimes we were interrupted by a villager requiring medical assistance. Budi was never impatient with the interruption but instead would help me to finish up so that we could go back to enjoying our evening. Years passed with this same routine of which I never tired. To many it might seem dull or boring, but to me it represented the stability and comfort I did not enjoy during the first half of my life. I could not picture myself this fulfilled and content anywhere else.

The most pleasant diversion from the usual routine was when Amri would come home from university and tell tales of meeting famous lecturers from around the world and sharing the harmless pranks and antics of his friends. During his second year, he decided he wanted to be an aeronautical engineer. Robert Gross, CEO of Lockheed Corporation, had visited the school and talked about the need for engineers in this growing field. My heart stopped. Amri was wide-eyed with excitement over the thought of building airplanes that could be used for the military and commercial flight. What Amri had no way of knowing was that I once knew Mr. Gross well. His staff had helped build the L-10 Electra airplane that Noonan and I used on our ill-fated trip.

On the outside I showed enthusiasm for Amri's decision, but on the inside, a new incarnation of the old worry invaded my idyllic existence. Budi listened intently to Amri's description of the coursework he would need to take to become an engineer, all the while watching for my reaction. Laying in Budi's arms that night I whispered my obvious concerns about Amri going into the field of aviation, even as an engineer.

Certainly he would eventually learn of Amelia Earhart and, with his intelligence, would quickly put two-and-two together. Budi assured me that whatever was to happen in the future was not something I should spend time worrying about in the present. "If there is nothing to worry about and you continue to worry, you will waste your time," he explained. "If you worry and there is something to worry about, it will do no good." Without minimizing my fears he logically suggested that I had only two options – to wait until (or if) Amri found out who I really was and then to explain my reasoning for keeping it a secret from him or to reveal the truth in the near future. I fell asleep that night with a heavy heart considering the ramifications of each choice.

After a fitful night's sleep I decided that Budi was right. It would do no good to worry about something out of my control. At this point in his life, it would only burden and confuse Amri were he to learn that the woman he knew as Meely was in fact someone else. Unless he asked, I would wait until he was older and finished with school before telling him my well-guarded secret.

The Beginning of the End

I believe that people see what they want to see. As Amri studied to become an aeronautical engineer, he no doubt learned about Amelia Earhart. But to him I was just Meely, the woman who nurtured and loved him from the time he was a small child. He needed me to be Meely. The villagers needed someone to tend to their illnesses and wounds, and so they saw me as a healer. And the world in the early 1930s needed a female heroine who they believed to be a great aviator – and that's what they saw.

Perhaps the mystery surrounding my disappearance entertained some, and so they did not want to know what really happened. In retrospect I believe those who wanted to could have learned of my existence. For all I know G.P. found some way to capitalize on the mystery. How many people have I come into contact with over the past twenty years who could have recognized me but instead chose to believe I was as I presented myself? In this way we are all, to some degree, who others need us to be at the moment. But the tragedy is losing oneself in being for others without thought for one's own needs. Fortunately for me I had the grand opportunity to reinvent myself as I wanted to be and as I wanted to be known.

I cannot help but think that many women would like to have this opportunity. Even today as women's roles in society are changing, they continue to bear the burden of caring for family and elderly parents alongside of any duties they may have outside the home. Yes, I chose a drastic path – to remain in obscurity even when I could have returned to my old life. I wonder, though, which is worse. That choice or to live a life you chose but no longer want?

I never had the chance to reveal myself to Amri. Upon graduating from college in 1956 he found a job in Lockheed's military aircraft plant in Prestwick, Scotland. Fluency in English combined with a brilliant mind and good grades made him an attractive hire to the company. Just as I was fearful for him to walk the streets of Jakarta on our first visit in 1950, then saddened by his departure for university, I was fearful to have him leave his homeland and go somewhere so far away. But he was so proud and full of enthusiasm for his new life that I could not help but encourage him to seek his destiny. As I once read in a book, *our children are not our children, they are the sons and daughters of life longing for itself.*

Amri spent the summer after college at home with us. How joyful I was to have him close once again. Budi found a job for him at his company so that he could learn the realities of working in a large corporation before leaving for Scotland. Over dinner he would pepper Budi with questions about the intricacies of various facets of his experiences. Most nights, engaged in their conversation about things and people of which I had no knowledge, I think they forgot I was even there! But it did not disturb me. Inside I felt once again whole and thoroughly satisfied.

One Saturday just before he was to leave for Scotland, Amri was helping me to clean the clinic when he brought up the subject of Buyat Bay. Rarely since our departure from the village did he discuss his childhood memories. As he focused on washing some utensils he said he wanted to thank me for saving him from what his life would have been had he remained there. He talked about our visit to the village, and I was surprised to learn that he experienced the same sense of guilt as I did for having left behind the poor children who eventually went to work in the mines. When I walked over to give him a hug he accepted it, but uncomfortably. He was a man now and was less patient with my demonstrations of affection.

It was during this conversation that Amri suggested I start a school for the poor children of Subang. He explained that without English he could not possibly have the same opportunities available to him. He talked about his friends at university who were smart, but were not fluent in English. He felt strongly that my earliest classes in English provided him with the foundation he needed to achieve his dreams. I promised I would give it thought and let him know what I decided. By that time I was nearly sixty years old and uncertain that I had the stamina or desire to undertake a new endeavor.

Nearly four years to the day after I bid Amri good-bye when he departed for university, I stood in the same place on another September morning and once again was faced with his departure. This time it made me melancholy, but didn't have the same devastating effect. I would always worry about the well-being of my boy, but this was the next stage of his journey. It was his journey, not mine. Even with this knowledge, nothing could prepare me for what was to follow.

On April 30, 1956, Budi came home early from the office. Although the office was quite close, it was unusual for him to return midday. He found me in the clinic and asked me to come to the house. He was uncharacteristically sedate as we sat together on the couch in our living room. I could not imagine what he wanted to tell me, but I knew from the ashen look on his face that it could not be good. Taking my hand, he explained that Amri was on a flight en route to Malta from London when his plane crashed as the result of pilot error. A chill like no other that I ever experienced overtook my body. I began to quake and could not stop. I cannot remember what else Budi said after he whispered that Amri had died.

MAKING PEACE

I do not know whether the recounting of Amri's passing or my own declining health has prevented me from writing for the past two weeks. If I were a more spiritual person I would believe that Amri was taken from me in punishment for my taking the life of Fred Noonan through my own error and arrogance.

Anyone who has ever lost a child knows the devastating and never-ending pain that must be endured for the rest of one's life. I am no different. To this day I see his smiling face before me when I close my eyes to rest. I smell the sweet aroma of his skin when I take a deep breath. I feel his farewell embrace as I lay in bed at night. In an effort to keep a picture of him clearly painted in my mind, I will myself to recall the most minute details of our lives together. Sometimes there are still tears. At other times anger takes their place.

I know I do not deserve to escape life's inevitable losses, but I wonder why my dear Amri had to be taken when he was so young, so full of promise. I know there could not be a God for he would not have me save the life of a boy only to take him away before he could make his own mark on the world. As I near the end of my own life, I hope that I am wrong and that indeed there is a heaven and I will once again be united with my sweet boy.

I would not think it possible, but after Amri's death Budi and I became even closer. He retired from his job to spend more time with me. In the weeks and months immediately following Amri's passing I could not bring myself to do the most routine things to which I was accustomed. Instead Budi and I took long walks and occasional trips to Bandung or Jakarta to visit with Arida. I was no longer fearful of having my identity discovered. There was little more I had to lose. My anonymity no longer seemed as important as it once did. Looking back, I even felt a bit foolish at having for so long made it such a central part of my existence. Why did I not simply let the chips fall where they may? If discovered, I could have explained that I wished to maintain my privacy. I could have been honest. But when we are young we make issues out of things that later in life seem so much less consequential.

It was in Bandung that I could most feel Amri's presence. Budi showed me where he stayed and studied. The most painful part was when we would encounter one of Amri's professors. The inevitable question about how their star student was doing led to an explanation of what had happened to him. Budi did the explaining as I stood by silently.

Not long after, Arida retired and began spending long week-ends with us. Tuti became an invaluable help to us all and was so much more than just a servant. She was a member of our family. Arida surprised us on one of her visits by bringing along several guests – Cinta and her daughter Itje! Now the self-confident mother of a five-year-old, Cinta and I stayed awake long into the night catching up on our lives in the intervening years since we had see one another. She told me about marrying the woodworker from the village and how he died in an automobile accident when Itje was just two years old. I asked her about my friends in Kamanta and she proudly informed me that she had passed on her knowledge of herbal medicine to her own servant who could now work independently with the villagers requiring attention. It made me happy to think that Santi's work was continuing decades later for what I hoped would be decades to come.

The night before Cinta was to leave, I asked Budi whether we should invite her to come and live with us. I was getting older and needed someone to provide more assistance than Tuti was capable of. He could see me begin to blossom in the presence of my old protégé and readily agreed that if Cinta wanted to, she and Itje could remain with us as long as they would like. Much to my delight, Cinta agreed. She wanted her daughter to be educated and knew that the schools in Subang were more advanced than those in Kamanta.

Our home was once again filled with youth and energy. Together Cinta and I resumed our former pattern of growing and mixing herbs and tending to those who came for help. Like her mother, Itje was a clever girl with a kind spirit. She attended a local school, made friends, and quickly adapted to her new life in Subang. Our dinner table was always filled with lively conversation of three generations unrelated by blood but in all other ways a family bonded together by love.

THE AMRI SCHOOL

In the early 1960s, I was approached by one of the Indonesian executives from Anglo Indonesian Plantation, Ltd. and asked to help establish a school for teaching English to the children of the native workers who lived in the village. I recalled Amri's same suggestion during one of our last conversations. By now I was over 60 years old and slowing down considerably. I was not certain that I had the energy to start a school, or to help children learn my native language. I expressed my hesitation, but the executive was insistent and passionate about the need for the children to learn English so that they could have more choices in life than simply following in the footsteps of their parents who worked in the factory or fields doing manual labor. I promised that I would consider his proposal and let him know of my decision.

Budi, Cinta and I discussed the idea for several weeks. As always, Budi had only my best interests in mind and said that he would support me regardless of the decision I made. He did, however, offer to help me in any way he could and, if I would show him how to do so, agreed to be a teacher in the school. Cinta was more enthusiastic about the idea. She assured me that she and Tuti could handle the clinic if that was of concern to me.

I thought about Amri and heard his childlike voice as he practiced reading his books aloud in English. I also thought about the children of Buyat Bay who were just beginning to become proficient in English when Amri and I left. These thoughts helped me to make the decision that I could not turn my back on these children. With the help of Budi, I began preparations for the first English language school in Subang.

The company was helpful in securing the books and supplies needed for the school. They loaned several workers to build a one-room schoolhouse on land they owned and promised to provide on-going financial assistance to hire new teachers as it grew. Once the school was built and the supplies had arrived, we held a Saturday open house for residents of Subang. Before we opened the doors to the parents and children waiting outside, Budi, Cinta, and Tuti presented me with a gift. It was an intricately carved wooden sign with gold painted letters to hang on the front of the school: The Amri School of English.

Those who visited the school that Saturday came more out of curiosity than commitment, but soon we had filled the classroom to capacity. We began with me teaching the youngest children the basics, and then Budi took over once the children became older and had a firmer grasp of the English language. Budi proved to be a wonderful teacher beloved by the students. He reminded me of his father. In my sixth decade I had returned to working with children in much the same way as I had with Dennison House in Boston so many years ago. My life had come full circle.

The school had been in operation for nearly three years when Budi complained of chest pains that would not go away. He was increasingly short of breath and grew tired quickly. Cinta offered to spend days at the school and evenings at the clinic so that Budi and I could travel to Jakarta to see a heart specialist. After spending five days at Arida's home and going through a battery of tests, the doctor gravely informed us that Budi was suffering from congestive heart failure. There was no cure for the condition, but Budi's life could be prolonged if he would carefully guard his energy and not exert himself.

Hand-in-hand, we rode silently back to Subang. After taking care of me for so long, it was now my turn to take care of Budi. We each were lost in our own private thoughts of what the future would bring for us. Although the ride was only a few hours, it seemed like an eternity as I looked out the window trying to hold back my tears. I could not imagine my life without Budi. I remembered an Emily Dickinson poem that I read while at Denison House:

"My life closed twice before its close;
It yet remains to see
If Immortality unveil
A third event to me,
So huge, so hopeless to conceive,
As these that twice befell.
Parting is all we know of heaven,
And all we need of hell."

I instinctively knew that this would soon be true for me as well.

Losing Budi

Within a few months, Budi's condition deteriorated, and he became tired and weak. It took all of his strength to walk from the bedroom to the living room. I suggested that we travel to the U.S. where certainly we could get better, more advanced care. It was of no concern to me that my identity might be made public. I wanted only for Budi to be healthy once again. But Budi would not hear of it. Even in the end he felt the need to protect me.

Unlike the sudden shock of losing Amri, I had time to say my final good-byes to Budi in both words and deeds. I would spend a few hours at the school each day while Tuti stayed to keep an eye on him, then I would return to make him lunch and read to him from his favorite classical books. In the evening we would sit on the porch and watch the moon rise, a great light in the sky. How vividly I recall one evening when it was so full that it filled the sky with an orange glow – the most beautiful sight I had ever seen.

We talked about his mother, father, and Amri and his belief that he would be joined with them again in the hereafter. I shared with him my deepest feelings about our all too short but idyllic life together and thanked him for allowing me to know abiding love in my life. He instructed me what to do with his bodily remains and estate once he was gone, assuring me that I would be well taken care of and, more importantly, forever loved. When it was clear that the end was near and he could no longer get out of bed, I wrote to Arida and asked her to immediately come to Subang to be with us.

On the day that Arida arrived Budi had not woken up until late afternoon. When he saw his sister he smiled and reached out his hand to her. I backed out of the room to allow them time alone together. When Arida came out there were tears in her eyes. She put her head on my shoulder and wept. I held her close, trying hard to keep my own emotions in check so that I could be there for her, the sister who would soon have no blood relatives of her own – and not by her choosing.

We let Budi sleep and over dinner exchanged our favorite stories about him. Neither of us could eat each much, and so we finally left the table to sit on the porch in the cool evening air. She told me what it was like growing up with him as her brother in Kamanta and how he always protected her from the mean village children. Intermittently we cried and hugged and laughed, all the while knowing that our Budi would soon be gone.

That night I crawled into bed with Budi for the first time in several weeks. I did not want to disturb his sleep but I felt the need to be close to him. He stirred for a moment, put his arm out for me to come close and kissed me on the forehead. Emotionally exhausted I fell asleep in his arms only to awake at sunrise to the realization that he was gone.

I do not know what I would have done without Cinta, Arida, and Tuti. Even little Itje would try her best to comfort me. Just as the women of Buyat Bay came to my rescue when I arrived in their village, these dear women forged a protective circle to enable me to once again heal. They stayed close enough to remind me of their presence, yet distant enough to permit me to grieve in my own way. Cinta took over at the school while Tuti worked in the clinic. She had learned much from Cinta's patient tutelage.

I did not know how I could possibly survive the loss of Amri, but I did. In some strange way it prepared me for Budi's passing. I knew that life would go on, although the sunsets would never be quite as bright nor the moments of joy quite as fulfilling. Eventually I returned to teach at The Amri School of English. I oversaw its expansion from a one-room schoolhouse to a compound with nine classrooms, a kitchen, cafeteria, and office. I hired new teachers, trained them, and gradually withdrew from the classroom, spending more time managing the operations of the school.

Sleeping alone in the bed that Budi and I once shared never became easier. To this day I find myself reaching over to feel the warmth of his presence. Sometimes his presence is so tangible that I know he is near. It is always with a sense of deep disappointment when I awake from a dream where he and I are together only to find myself alone.

Last year Arida sold her home in Jakarta and came to live with us. Although she is several years older than me, she is in good health and keeps a watchful eye over the clinic, the school, and the servants. Tuti hovers over me like a mother hen. Sometimes I shooed her away needing respite from her concern. She wonders what it is that I have been so diligently committing to paper these past months. Several times I have seen her glance furtively at my papers, but her inability to read English prevents her from reading the words. If only she had taken me up on my offer to teach her English! Then her curiosity would be sated.

Having lived for so long with only women, first at Buyat Bay while men went on their long fishing expeditions, then with Santi and Amri, and finally with Budi, it brings me great comfort to be once again surrounded by women. We bring a different, but equally reassuring energy to the house. We offer one another support, love, and mutual respect for our individual gifts. As we pass our knowledge, history and wisdom from generation to generation, we continue the tradition of sisterhood in the truest sense of the word. I learned to be a sister from Muriel, but I learned sisterhood from my friends.

My Story Ends

I suppose it is normal that as one nears the end of life she inventories her decisions, actions, and relationships. In my case, I feel compelled to set the record straight. I have tried to make up for the hurt I caused others by leading a life devoted to helping those more vulnerable than I. I have been privileged in so many ways, and to hoard that abundance would be selfish beyond comprehension. I have stumbled along the way and not met the needs of everyone who has asked for my assistance, but finally I can admit, I am only human. Had I been able to do that earlier, my life may have turned out very different.

Having told my story the best I can, it's now time to let go of the past once and for all. It has become more and more difficult to write as my stamina has diminished. Surely there is more that I can say, but there are no words left. I never was one for minute details. They bore me. I paint my canvas with broad strokes, so much more intrigued by breadth than depth. I was blessed to live two lives. One on an international stage and one in obscurity. Was one life *better* than the other? No. They were different. Had I not lived the former life the latter life would not have been possible.

Lately I cannot clear from my mind a poem that I memorized for a junior high school pageant that marked the passage into high school. How odd that I may not be able to recall what I did yesterday, but I can remember each and every word of the Robert Frost poem that I chose to recite, "The Road Not Taken." Like the Emily Dickinson poem that stuck with me for decades, this one certainly must have informed my life in some way. I should have known even then that my life would not be linear or usual. I do not consider myself an unusual person but my path has been far from what others might describe as typical.

"Two roads diverged in a yellow wood
And sorry I could not travel both
And be one traveler, long I stood
And looked down one as far as I could
To where it bent in the undergrowth.
Then took the other, as just as fair,
And having perhaps the better claim,
Because it was grassy and wanted wear,
Though as for that the passing there
Had worn them really about the same.
And both that morning equally lay
In leaves no step had trodden black.
Oh, I kept the first for another day!
Yet knowing how way leads to way,
I doubted if I should ever come back.
I shall be telling this with a sigh,
Somewhere ages and ages hence:
Two road diverged in a wood, and I --
I took the one less traveled by
And that has made all the difference."

I hope Budi was right and that it will not be long before I join Grandmother, Grandfather, Santi, Amri, and Budi. Perhaps by now I will also be joining Mama, Papa, and Muriel. I don't know. I would like to see the school and children one more time. And I have one final task to complete. I've asked Tuti to escort me to the school as I can no longer maneuver the distance alone. Once I wrap these pages in twine I will be ready to leave, having said all that I can about my road less traveled.

EPILOGUE

What you have just read is a fictionalized version of what might have become of Amelia Earhart after her disappearance. The facts prior to 1937 were meticulously researched to ensure I had a thorough understanding of what it might have been like to be Amelia Earhart. But the story subsequent to 1937 was born in my imagination, considering the fact that her remains have never been decisively identified. Reading every book and newspaper article available about Amelia, as well as watching documentaries about her life, I came to realize that like many women she may have felt overwhelmed with the responsibilities of family and notoriety. If she survived, she might well have chosen to live the remainder of her life in obscurity, albeit not isolation.

How many of us have wished we could disappear? I recall sitting by a pool one summer afternoon speaking with my niece, newly married and with a step-child, telling me she sometimes wished she could vanish. When my housekeeper's sister was dying of cancer, I held her as she said she sobbed on my shoulder that she wished she could just disappear and that this would all prove to be a bad dream. And when I shared this manuscript with my dear friend Josh, he told me about the time his mother vanished for a week, overwhelmed with the responsibility of two young sons and a busy husband. Later I learned from other women that they had similar experiences with their own mothers.

The fantasy of boarding an airplane to Provence, Tuscany, or even Subang and living my final years in the seclusion of the countryside they provide is tremendously appealing. The thought of starting fresh and removing myself from the burdens of modern life in the United States captures my imagination and remains ever present in my mind. I weigh the thought of leaving loved ones with the appeal of crafting a life free from responsibility. And I am not yet convinced that one of these locales will not become my own alternate flight plan.

What I wish readers to take away from this story is the knowledge that they themselves are faced with choice points that define their lives. None of us escape from the existential burden of creating a life of meaning. Too often we accept our lot in life without questioning what we might do to create a more meaningful existence. It is always a choice and there is always a consequence. The question of whether you are willing to assume the responsibility concomitant with the choice will determine your ultimate existence.

I leave you with the following questions to consider. I cannot possibly tell you what is right for you, but your answers to these questions may point you to your destiny:

- Do you think Amelia was courageous or cowardly in her decision to live in anonymity? Why?
- Should Amelia have returned to the United States? Why?
- Could Amelia have made a bigger impact on the lives of more people had she returned to the U.S. rather than remain in Indonesia living as Meely?
- If you were in Amelia's situation, what would you have done?
- In what ways can you compare your life with Amelia's before her disappearance?
- In what ways does Meely's story resonate with you?
- What are some of the things you tolerate in current relationships or situations that are detrimental to your well-being? What are you willing to do differently?
- How would you describe an ideal life? What actions can you take to move toward it?
- What are some ways in which Meely made a lasting contribution to the lives of those she encountered on her journey?
- What is the significance of the women in Meely's life? The men? How was that different from the significance of the men and women in Amelia's life before her disappearance?
- What lessons had Meely not learned at the time of her death?
- If you could sit with Amelia and ask her one question, what would it be? How would the answer change *your* life?

Resources

The following books and DVDs are recommended to learn more about the fascinating life of Amelia Earhart:

- **Amelia: A Life of the Aviation Legend,** Donald M. Goldstein and Katherine V. Dillon (Brassey's, 1997).
- **Amelia Earhart,** Doris L. Rich (Smithsonian Press, 1996).
- **Finding Amelia**, Ric Gillespie (U.S. Naval Institute Press, 2006).
- **20 Hours, 40 Min: Our Flight in the Friendship**, Amelia Earhart (National Geographic, 2003).
- **The Sound of Wings: The Life of Amelia Earhart**, Mary S. Lovell (St. Martin's Griffin, 1991).
- **Biography: Amelia Earhart** (A&E DVD Archives, 2005).
- **Amelia Earhart: The Final Flight** (Turner Home Entertainment, 1994).
- **Amelia: The Tale of Two Sisters** (Netflix, 2017)

ABOUT THE AUTHOR

Alternate Flight Plan: The Lost Diary of Amelia Earhart is Dr. Lois Frankel's first work of fiction. Her previous books, **Nice Girls Don't Get the Corner Office** and **Nice Girls Don't Get Rich** are *New York Times* and *Wall Street Journal* bestsellers. Other books include **Nice Girls Just Don't Get** (written with Carol Frohlinger), **See Jane Lead, Stop Sabotaging Your Career** and **Ageless Women, Timeless Wisdom**. Lois has appeared on the TODAY Show, CNN, Larry King Live, 20/20 and CNBC as well as being featured in the *New York Times*, *USA Today*, and in *People* and *Time* magazines. As an internationally recognized public speaker she is sought after for her witty and practical presentations that actively engage the audience

Lois is President of Corporate Coaching International, a California consulting firm. Her client list of leading business organizations includes Amgen, ARCO Indonesia, Boeing, Lockheed Martin, McKinsey, Nestle, Northrop Grumman, and Procter and Gamble. Among Dr. Frankel's outstanding accomplishments is the founding two nonprofit organizations, Bloom Again Foundation and Motivating Our Students Through Experience (MOSTE). Maybelline New York recognized her efforts with their Empowerment Through Education Award and a $10,000 grant to MOSTE.

Originally from New York, Dr. Frankel now calls Southern California home. Apart from her extensive writing, speaking, and coaching activities, she describes herself as an avid photographer, average golfer, and enthusiastic bicyclist.

22765201R00070

Made in the USA
Columbia, SC
01 August 2018